TRANSLATED CHRISTIANITIES

...padre Fray Alon-
...Molina, sant Francis-
...pirqui: ynipan oquimo
...ti ennahuatlatolli.

...atolpeuhcayotl .

...dre fray Alonso de Mo...
...dela orden del señor sant
...cisco, traduzido en lengua
los nauas por el mismo a...

¶ Prologo.

TRANSLATED CHRISTIANITIES

Nahuatl and Maya Religious Texts

Mark Z. Christensen

The Pennsylvania State University Press
University Park, Pennsylvania

Portions of chapter 1 previously appeared in "The Use of Nahuatl in Evangelization and the Ministry of Sebastian," *Ethnohistory* 59, no. 4 (2012): 691–711. Copyright 2012, American Society for Ethnohistory. All rights reserved. Reprinted by permission of the publisher, Duke University Press (www.dukeupress .edu). Material from chapter 1 also appeared in "The Tales of Two Cultures: Ecclesiastical Texts and Nahua and Maya Catholicisms," *The Americas* 66, no. 3 (2010): 353–77.

Library of Congress Cataloging-in-Publication Data
Christensen, Mark Z., author.
Translated Christianities : Nahuatl and Maya religious texts / Mark Z. Christensen.
    p.   cm—(Latin American originals ; 8)
Summary: "English translations of Nahuatl and Maya religious texts, including sermons, catechisms, and confessional manuals. Includes commentary examining the various Christianities presented to the colonial Aztec (Nahua) and Yucatec Maya, the origins and purpose of the texts, and their authors and the messages they intended to convey"—Provided by publisher.
Includes bibliographical references and index.
ISBN 978-0-271-06361-4 (pbk. : alk. paper)
1. Aztecs—Religion.
2. Mayas—Religion.
3. Christian literature, Spanish—Translations into Nahuatl.
4. Christian literature, Spanish—Translations into Maya.
5. Christianity and culture—Mexico—History.
I. Title. II. Series: Latin American originals ; 8.

F1219.76.R45C54 2014
299.7'8452—dc23
2013046801

To Cade

whose smile needs no translation

CONTENTS

Latin American Originals (LAO) is a series of primary source texts on colonial Latin America. LAO volumes are accessible, affordable editions of texts translated into English—most of them for the very first time. Of the eight volumes now in print, five illuminate aspects of the Spanish conquests during the long century of 1494–1614, and three push our understandings of the spiritual conquest into surprising new territories.

Taken in the chronological order of their primary texts, LAO 7 comes first. *Of Cannibals and Kings* presents the very earliest written attempt to describe the native cultures of the Americas. An early ethnography, written by a Catalan named Ramón Pané, is packaged with complementary Spanish texts about the Caribbean societies of the late 1490s. Together they offer startling new insight into how the first Europeans in the Americas struggled from the very start to conceive a New World.

Following the chronological sequence of their source materials, LAO 2 comes next. *Invading Guatemala* shows how reading multiple accounts of conquest wars (in this case, Spanish, Nahua, and Maya versions of the Guatemalan conflict of the 1520s) can explode established narratives and suggest a conquest story that is more complicated, disturbing, and revealing. LAO 1, *Invading Colombia*, challenges us to view the difficult Spanish invasion of Colombia in the 1530s as more representative of conquest campaigns than the better-known assaults on the Aztec and Inca empires.

LAO 3, *The Conquest on Trial*, features a fictional embassy of native Americans filing a complaint over the conquest in a court in Spain—the Court of Death. That text, the first theatrical examination of the conquest published in Spain, effectively condensed contemporary debates on colonization into one dramatic package. LAO 4, *Defending the Conquest*, is a spirited, ill-humored, and polemic apologia for the Spanish Conquest written by Bernardo de Vargas

Machuca, a lesser-known veteran conquistador, and submitted for publication—without success—in 1613.

Volumes 5, 6, and 8 all explore aspects of Spanish efforts to implant Christianity in the New World. LAO 5, *Forgotten Franciscans*, casts new light on the spiritual conquest and the conflictive cultural world of the Inquisition in sixteenth-century Mexico. Both it and LAO 6 show how there were wildly divergent views within the church in Spanish America both on native religions and on how to replace them with Christianity. *Gods of the Andes* presents the first English edition of a 1594 manuscript describing Inca religion and the campaign to convert native Andeans. Its Jesuit author, Blas Valera, is surprisingly sympathetic to pre-conquest beliefs and practices, viewing them as preparing Andeans for the arrival of the faith he helped bring from Spain.

In this new offering, LAO 8, *Translated Christianities*, Mark Christensen presents religious texts in Nahuatl and Yucatec Maya, which he himself has translated into English. Designed to help proselytize and ensure the piety of indigenous parishioners in central Mexico and Yucatan, these texts show how such efforts actually contributed to the development of local Christianities. As in other parts of the Americas, native cultures thrived within the conversion process, leading to fascinatingly multifaceted outcomes.

The source texts to LAO volumes are either archival documents—written in European languages, most obviously Spanish, or indigenous languages, such as Nahuatl and Maya—or rare books published in the colonial period in their original language. The contributing authors are historians, anthropologists, and scholars of literature; they have developed a specialized knowledge that allows them to locate, translate, and present these texts in a way that contributes to scholars' understanding of the period, while also making them readable for students and non-specialists.

In that varied firmament, Mark Christensen is a rising star. A historian comfortable working with sources in multiple languages, including two Mesoamerican tongues, he has already published a groundbreaking monograph, titled *Nahua and Maya Catholicisms*, that acts as LAO 8's hefty sibling. As Mark received his PhD at Penn State, it is serendipitously appropriate for his work to contribute to the evolution of the LAO series.

—Matthew Restall

FIGURES AND TABLES

ACKNOWLEDGMENTS

This book is the product of a variety of other research projects. Those scholars who spend hours and hours translating texts know too well the disappointment of having to omit the translations from the final project due to word count limits or other editorial decisions. I myself had collected a variety of translations from Nahuatl and Maya religious texts that I never thought would see the light of day but that I frequently made copies of and distributed to my students in an effort to provide examples of the texts themselves. Matthew Restall first suggested that I work the translations into a book for the Latin American Originals series, and I am extremely grateful for his encouragement, without which these translations would still be computer files or, in other cases, untranslated manuscripts. Ellie Goodman, the executive editor of the Penn State University Press, has also provided valuable guidance along the way.

The translations in this book benefited from the advice and critique of others more expert than me. First and foremost, James Lockhart has generously provided me with his assistance, suggestions, and support. He is a valued mentor, and his aid with the Nahuatl translations proved invaluable to this project; I am profoundly grateful. Matthew Restall also deserves my sincerest thanks for his input not only on the Maya texts but on the book in general. He was always willing to read a chapter (or two or three) and offer helpful advice. I value his friendship. I also presented select translations at the 2011 and 2012 Northeastern Group of Nahuatl Studies Conference at Yale, where they benefited from the collective insight, expertise, and enthusiasm of those scholars attending. Stafford Poole also deserves thanks for his help with translating the Latin passages, as does Louise Burkhart for her insights into Nahuatl religious vocabulary, and Fr. Roger Corriveau for his assistance with all things

Catholic. In the end, I assume sole responsibility for the translations and any errors or misrepresentations.

Many have encouraged this project along the way, and I am grateful for every kind word of support. My particular thanks goes to Victoria Bricker, Todd Christensen, John F. Chuchiak, Michael Francis, Rebecca Horn, Ben Leeming, Martin Nesvig, Caterina Pizzigoni, Stafford Poole, A. Gregg Roeber, Susan Schroeder, John F. Schwaller, John Sullivan, and Jon Truitt. In many ways, the research and scholarship of others have paved the way to this book. The list is too large to include here, but all those who have endeavored to expand our understanding of colonial Latin America through native-language texts have my gratitude.

I would also like to thank those who facilitated my discovery and acquisition of many of the texts appearing in this book: Msgr. José Camargo Sosa at the Archivo Histórico del Arzobispado de Yucatán, Elizabeth Gano Sørenssen at the Schøyen Collection, Hortensia Calvo at the Latin American Library at Tulane, and the staff at both the Tozzer Library at Harvard University and the Department of Rare Books and Special Collections at Princeton University Library. The John Carter Brown Library also deserves praise for its wonderful collection of digitized Nahuatl texts made available online, as does the Department of History at Assumption College for its financial support. Finally, I am indebted to Gretchen Whalen for her pioneering transcription and translation of the Morley Manuscript, which brought to light a valuable piece of colonial Maya literature.

Academia can drown you if you are not careful, so I am most grateful for my personal lifeguards: my wife, Natalie, and three children, Macy, Cade, and Carter. Thank you for holding my head above water by keeping my perspectives and priorities focused on those things in life that matter most.

Mesoamerica. Map by Chris Becker.

All English translations of the Nahuatl and Maya texts are my own. Parts of my translation in chapter 1 have appeared in my articles with *The Americas* and *Ethnohistory* and are used here with permission.[1] This is the first time the English translation of the sermon has appeared in its entirety as presented in the original manuscript. Regarding the Maya stories in chapter 2, Gretchen Whalen, who first examined the Morley Manuscript from which the stories derive, posted her English translation of the entire manuscript (including the Maya stories) to the website of the Foundation for the Advancement of Mesoamerican Studies (FAMSI).[2] Here, I have provided my own translations of the stories and juxtapose them with their medieval archetypes to better expose their transition into a colonial Maya world. The translations found in chapters 3, 4, and 5 have never seen publication anywhere.

I have made every effort to make the English translations readable. Thus, oftentimes I favor a figurative rather than a literal translation of the texts. Nahuatl and Maya texts generally omit punctuation, spacing, and paragraphing according to modern conventions, so I have included them. In instances of possible confusion, I use parentheses to convey intended meanings and brackets for omitted words. Occasionally, the native-language texts contain headings or brief sentences in Spanish; these appear translated in italics. Latin also appears at times in these texts, and I similarly translate such passages in italics but indicate their Latin origins in the notes.

---

1. Translations for the first half of the sermon that concern the conversion of Paul appear in Christensen, "Tales of Two Cultures"; translations for the second half of the sermon regarding the ministry of Sebastian appear in Christensen "Nahuatl in Evangelization."

2. Whalen, "Annotated Translation."

Introduction

Native-Language Religious Texts

Neither Castilian nor Latin . . . could more expressively persuade nor teach the mysteries of our Catholic religion than that which this [Nahuatl] work manifests.
—Carlos de Tapia Zenteno, in Ignacio de Paredes, *Promptuario manual mexicano*, 1759

It would be very useful to have printed books in the language of these Indians (Mayas) about Genesis and the creation of the world; because they have fables, or very harmful histories, and some of these they have written, and they guard them and read them in their meetings. And I had one of these copybooks that I confiscated from a *maestro* named Cuytun of the town of Sucopo, who escaped. And I could never have him to know the origin of this his Genesis.
—Pedro Sánchez de Aguilar, *Informe contra idolorum*, 1636

After years of hard work, Ignacio de Paredes submitted his book for publication. It was the year 1759, and the Jesuit priest was hopeful that his *Promptuario manual mexicano* would help Spanish priests preach the Christian message to the descendants of the Aztecs and the natives of central Mexico. The book was written in the Aztec language, Nahuatl, and its purpose was to provide ecclesiastics with a sermon or speech for every Sunday of the year; all the priest had to do was read from the manual every Sunday and the natives would learn the Christian doctrine. Carlos de Tapia Zenteno, who understood Nahuatl well, had the task of reviewing the book to ensure that it was free of any translation errors. He deemed the book and its conveyance of the doctrine in Nahuatl so eloquent that he claimed, "Neither Castilian nor Latin . . . could more expressively persuade nor teach the mysteries of our Catholic religion."

In early seventeenth-century Yucatan the secular priest Pedro Sánchez de Aguilar launched a campaign to rid his parish of its wooden and stone representations of ancient deities, or what the Spaniards saw as "idols." In the process, not only did he find numerous examples of the Mayas practicing idolatry, but, even worse, he found a number of handwritten Maya texts that blended Christian doctrine with precontact Maya beliefs. One case involved a Maya religious assistant—tasked, among other things, with the responsibility of teaching the doctrine—whose religious text conveyed an unorthodox Christian-Maya view of the Creation. To remedy the situation, Sánchez de Aguilar requested the publication of religious texts in Maya that accurately taught the doctrine. Without such books, he claimed that the Mayas "live without light."[1]

Both examples are representative in a number of ways. To begin, they illustrate the important role religious texts written in Nahuatl and Maya played in the evangelization of central Mexico and Yucatan. These books allowed ecclesiastics and their assistants to convey something of Christianity to the natives. These two examples, however, also demonstrate that texts could vary in their content and doctrinal accuracy. Some religious texts, like that of Paredes, conveyed Christianity in sufficiently orthodox ways, while others, like those Sánchez de Aguilar discovered, failed to do so. Thus, both examples represent two ends of a spectrum with orthodox native-language religious texts on one end, unorthodox texts on the other, and other Nahuatl and Maya texts somewhere in between.

This book provides the reader with the historical context and English translations of a few of the Nahuatl and Maya religious texts that conveyed the Christian doctrine to the Nahuas of central Mexico and the Yucatec Mayas. The purpose of doing so is threefold. First and foremost, these translations will give the English speaker access to the texts that conveyed Christianity to the natives. Native-language religious texts—sermons, confessional manuals, catechisms, and so on—were instrumental in the evangelization of Mexico and Yucatan. Yet the vast majority of these texts remain hidden to the modern reader, shrouded in general anonymity and the difficulty of translating native languages.[2] This book addresses this problem by

1. Sánchez de Aguilar, *Informe contra idolorum*, 181.
2. Some English translations would be Alva, *Guide to Confession*; Burkhart, *Holy Wednesday*; Burkhart, *Before Guadalupe*; Burkhart and Sell, *Nahuatl Theater*; Christensen, *Nahua and Maya Catholicisms*; Christensen, "Tales of Two Cultures"; and Christensen, "Nahuatl in Evangelization." For Maya, see Hanks, *Converting Words*. Gretchen Whalen has done significant work on Maya religious texts. In particular, see her "Annotated Translation." For English publications of the Chilam Balams, see chapter 2. Also, Nahuatl and Maya testaments and their religious preambles, although not didactic, can serve as religious texts. For the Nahua, see Cline

bringing to light a collection of religious texts in Nahuatl and Maya written between the 1550s and 1860s and gathered from archives throughout Mexico, Europe, and the United States.

The second purpose of this book is to illustrate the diversity of religious texts and their messages. To do so, it brings together English translations of Nahuatl and Maya texts of a similar genre (i.e., catechisms, confessional manuals, sermons) or that discuss a similar theme. This uncommon presentation of the translated texts is necessary for comparative insights into the Nahuatl and Maya works themselves, including authorial influence and their cultural, regional, and temporal adaptations. In a larger sense, a collection of translated Nahuatl and Maya religious texts offers a keener, more comprehensive understanding of the evangelization efforts made in central Mexico and Yucatan.

But evangelization efforts among native peoples were not monopolized by Catholics. Protestant faiths likewise utilized native-language religious texts to aid their proselytization—a largely unstudied fact due to the dearth of surviving works. This book provides a rare glimpse at the Methodist efforts to convert the Yucatec Mayas through a nineteenth-century Methodist catechism translated into Maya. The Methodist tract joins the other texts to enhance our appreciation of the diverse Christian messages native-language texts conveyed.

The third and final purpose of this book is to highlight the range in orthodoxy of religious texts from true and faithful representations of the Faith, to culturally modified redactions of Christianity. Although friars and priests composed religious texts, natives trained in religion and writing also put pen to paper. As a result, many of the texts translated in this book provide insights into how Christian doctrine changed according to the preferences and contributions of both Spanish and native authors. This, combined with the regional, temporal, cultural, and even denominational differences, all gave variety to Nahuatl and Maya religious texts and their translated Christianities.

---

and León-Portilla, *Testaments of Culhuacan,* and Pizzigoni, *Testaments of Toluca.* For the Maya, see Roys, *Titles of Ebtun,* and Restall, *Life and Death.* For more on testaments as religious texts, see Ramos, *Death and Conversion,* 114–15; and Christensen, *Nahua and Maya Catholicisms,* 84, 93–94.

Religious Texts

Didactic religious texts extend their roots back to the early stages of Christianity. Consider Augustine's fourth- and fifth-century *De doctrina christiana*, composed to facilitate an accurate comprehension and teaching of Christian doctrine and the homilies and sermons of the High Middle Ages. By the late fifteenth century the humanism of the Renaissance was sweeping across Europe, calling for reform and renewal through biblical studies and orthodox liturgy. Figures such as Martin Luther and Ulrich Zwingli and the subsequent Reformation fanned the flames of reform that illustrated, among other ideas, the need for individuals to have a basic understanding of Christian doctrine. For their part, Protestants generally desired individuals to gain personal understandings of the doctrine through vernacular translations of religious texts, including the Bible. The Catholic Church likewise recognized the need to successfully educate its fold and addressed such issues in the Council of Trent (1545–63). But the translation of scripture into the vernacular remained restricted, and the responsibility for the laity's education primarily fell to ecclesiastics. Trent ordered, for example, that "the bishop shall see to it that on Sundays and other festival days, the children in every parish be carefully taught the rudiments of the Faith."[3]

The printing press was a key player in the reformation efforts of both Protestants and Catholics. Since the fifteenth century the printing press was heavily employed to produce didactic religious works intended to direct their audiences in the religion and practice the authors prescribed. Traditionally, the production of religious texts was done by the pen of ecclesiastics and theologians. These handwritten texts ranged from the ascetic treatise of John Climacus's *Spiritual Ladder* to the theological teachings of Thomas Aquinas's *Summa theologica* to the Sunday sermon of the local parish priest. Yet ecclesiastical officials had limited control over what was written and thus the content of the text. The printing press, however, provided the church an opportunity to screen the contents of any given work through an extensive editorial process that included a variety of endorsements and approvals from religious authorities.[4] In an early

---

3. Schroeder, *Canons and Decrees*, 196.
4. For more on the subject, see Nesvig, *Ideology and Inquisition*, and Christensen, *Nahua and Maya Catholicisms*, 57–59.

modern era of reform that emphasized an orthodox education of the doctrine, the printing press and its religious texts would play a large role—a situation aptly reflected in the Americas.

The ecclesiastics that arrived in Mexico in the 1520s and 1530s did not wait for an operational printing press (1539) to begin producing religious texts. Outnumbered and faced with the enormous task of converting natives in their own tongue, the early friars and their predecessors composed a variety of religious texts, including manuscript catechisms and sermons in Nahuatl, Maya, and other languages to convey basic Catholic prayers and doctrine. Some were translations of European works such as the mid-sixteenth-century Nahuatl translation of Thomas à Kempis's fifteenth-century *On the Imitation of Christ*.[5] Others were original compositions tailored to local needs such as an 1803 confessional manual written for a Yucatecan friar administering in the Maya parish of Tixcacalcupul.[6]

Although manuscript works continued to play an important role in religious instruction—particularly in Yucatan, which waited until 1813 for its printing press—ecclesiastical authorities increasingly threw their support behind the printing press to produce works that would unify the Catholic message in New Spain. For example, the small Nahuatl *doctrina* (book of Christian doctrine) of fray Alonso de Molina saw print in 1546, and subsequent Franciscans suggested that to maintain a consistent message, this be the only such doctrina used for the Aztecs (or Nahuas).[7] Nevertheless, many other doctrinas followed, as did many confessional manuals, books of sermons, manuals detailing how to perform the sacraments, and myriad other Nahuatl and Maya religious texts. Different from one another, each text claimed to be the best of its kind and to convey the doctrine in the most effective manner. Simply put, although the printing press succeeded in making religious texts more available, it was unable to unify the message.

Nor was the printing press able to completely replace the production of handwritten native-language religious texts. Despite the

5. Tavárez, *Invisible War*, 28–29.

6. "Modo de confesar en lengua maya," item 26, col. 700, Rare Books and Manuscripts Library, University of Pennsylvania, Philadelphia.

7. *Códice franciscano*, 54. Scholars typically prefer the term "Nahua" over "Aztec" for a variety of reasons, not the least of which is that the latter term is generally used to represent only the Mexica. On the other hand, "Nahua" represents the Mexica and all other native cultures in central Mexico that shared the common language of Nahuatl.

increased availability of printed works, ecclesiastics and their native aides throughout the colonial period continued to generate manuscripts tailored to personal preferences and local demands. Some of these texts were handwritten "xeroxes" of printed originals; others represented original compositions. Some contained orthodox teachings; others did not. Because these texts avoided the quality control measures established for printed texts, ecclesiastical authorities were wary of the messages they contained. Certain ecclesiastical authorities and the Inquisition alike recognized the dangers of manuscript texts and confiscated them when discovered.[8] For example, in the 1570s Gerónimo del Alamo had a variety of works translated into Nahuatl, including a doctrina, confiscated from him because they were "de mano . . . [y] sin autor" (handwritten and anonymous).[9]

Another shortcoming of the printing press was its inability to reach Yucatan. To be sure, religious texts in Maya saw print through the presses in central Mexico, but in numbers that paled in comparison to their Nahuatl counterparts. Whereas Mexican ecclesiastics commonly complained of the abundance of different religious texts, Yucatecan ecclesiastics lamented the shortage of texts. In 1620 Juan Gómez Pacheco encouraged the publication of fray Juan Coronel's *Discursos predicables* because there was nothing printed in Maya for priests to use in instructing the natives.[10] The lack of printed works in Maya contributed to two consequences. First, the Christian religious education of the general Yucatec Maya population progressed more gradually than that of the Nahuas, allowing the 1722 Yucatecan synod to exclaim that the Yucatec Mayas were "the most barbarous" and possessed few signs of being Christians.[11] Second, handwritten manuscripts abounded in Yucatan to assist the local priests and to make up for the lack of printed works.[12]

The abundance of printed works in central Mexico and their dearth in Yucatan reflects a larger model of evangelization that

---

8. Burkhart, *Holy Wednesday*, 165; Acuña, "Escritos mayas inéditos," 168–69; Tavárez, *Invisible War*, 71–3, 129–58; Nesvig, *Ideology and Inquisition*, 134–63.

9. Fernández del Castillo, *Libros y libreros*, 488.

10. Coronel, *Discursos predicables*, xii–xiii.

11. Gómez de Parada, *Constituciones sinodales*, 39. See also Francisco Eugenio Domínguez y Argáiz's opinion in his *Pláticas*, preliminary leaf, unnumbered.

12. See, for example, the observations of José María Meneses in Ruz, *Colección de sermones*, 9–10.

favored the centers over peripheries.[13] Comparatively speaking, unlike in central Mexico, the conquest and settlement of Yucatan was a long, protracted event that postponed the stable presence of ecclesiastics. This delay, along with Yucatan's location as a periphery to the fast-growing Spanish center in central Mexico, affected the evangelization efforts of ecclesiastics while increasing the autonomy of the Mayas. Consider that in Yucatan, by the end of the colonial period, only approximately 37 percent of the 215 Maya towns had resident priests.[14] Generally speaking, although Christianity came to the Yucatec Maya, it did so at a slower pace than that seen in central Mexico, and Nahuatl and Maya religious texts bear the evidence.

Authors and Ghostwriters

Thus far, we have discussed the importance of native-language religious texts in the evangelization of the Nahuas and Mayas, their printed and manuscript forms, and their relative abundance among the Nahuas vis-à-vis the Mayas. But who wrote these texts? The title pages of printed texts propose Spanish ecclesiastics as the sole authors. Yet upon closer examination of the historical record and the texts themselves, the contributions of Nahuas and Mayas as assistants, scribes, ghostwriters, and authors become increasingly apparent.

The plan of many of the early friars included the assistance of natives in composing religious tracts in native languages. In the sixteenth century the Franciscans viewed the religious education of the native youth as instrumental in their overall evangelization efforts. Generally speaking, every town was to have an elderly native collect the youth and deliver them to the church each morning to learn the fundamentals of the Christian doctrine, including the Persignum crucis, or Sign of the Cross, the Lord's Prayer, the Apostles' Creed, and other basics. Afterward, the children would return home and assist

---

13. Although a model of centers and peripheries provides a useful framework when speaking of generalities, its ability to prescribe outcomes is limited by exceptions. Surely there were Mayas who surpassed their Nahua counterparts in religious education despite their peripheral location. In *Magistrates of the Sacred*, Taylor provides a useful analysis, showing the abilities and limits of such a model (45–46).

14. Thompson, *Tekanto*, 17.

their parents in their various duties.[15] For the common Nahua and Maya, the level of religious instruction would end here with the basic fundamentals of the Faith.

According to the early Franciscans, however, the children of the Nahua and Maya elite had a separate destiny.[16] Towns with resident friars and convents (a religious house for either men or women) also typically had schools used to train the children of the native nobility. Prior to the arrival of the Spanish, the native nobility governed over the spiritual and temporal lives of their towns. To the friars, then, these individuals would continue to serve as rulers, but now as Christians setting a good example and promulgating the message. The children of the native nobility were destined for the schoolroom, where they learned the Christian doctrine and studied reading, writing, and a variety of other subjects that could include Latin, theology, and grammar. Most important, they learned how to assist ecclesiastics in their duties to confess, perform mass, and instruct.[17]

Some of these religiously trained native nobles would serve as cooks or groundskeepers in the convents and churches; others became singers, or sacristans. Still others returned to their towns to serve as surrogate priests—typically referred to as *fiscales* for the Nahuas and *maestros* for the Mayas—who would baptize, catechize, bless, and preach in the frequent absence of the priest. Those with a proven aptitude for reading and writing helped others in learning similar skills and assisted friars still novice in the language.[18] In fact, many early Spanish authors recognized the roles native assistants played in writing their texts. Fray Bernardino de Sahagún, himself an expert in the language, stated that such assistants "correct for us the incongruities we express in the sermons or write in the catechisms."[19] In his 1560s *Coloquios y doctrina cristiana*, Sahagún gives credit to the Nahuas Antonio Valeriano, Alonso Vegerano, Martín Jacobita, and Andrés Leonardo for their assistance.[20] Fray Juan Bautista also recog-

15. *Códice franciscano*, 56–57.

16. Indeed, the *Códice franciscano* records the Franciscan's displeasure with those who teach indifferently and who raise commoners to be rulers in their towns (55–57).

17. For a general treatment of the matter, see ibid., 55–70, and R. Ricard, *Spiritual Conquest*, 96–101. For more regarding the Yucatecan schools, see Molina Solís, *Historia de Yucatán*, 1:321–32; and Hanks, *Converting Words*, 59–84.

18. *Códice franciscano*, 57–62.

19. Sahagún, *Introductions and Indices*, 83–84.

20. Sahagún, *Coloquios y doctrina*, 75.

nized the native assistants that both he and Molina used to compose their works.[21] The situation in Yucatan was similar, where one Maya assistant, Gaspar Antonio Chi, stated, "[I] have taught the said friars . . . the language of these natives, which I interpret to them . . . and I have written sermons for them in the language to preach to the said natives."[22]

But the contributions of natives increasingly came under fire as the colonial period progressed and as precontact religious practices continued to persist in a Christian society. The First Mexican Provincial Council of 1555 claimed that due to the errors natives commit when translating religious texts and the misunderstandings conveyed, they were no longer allowed to translate or possess native-language sermons. If natives were to be given such texts, the texts themselves had to bear the signature of the ecclesiastic who gave it to them.[23] The council then stipulated that native-language religious texts required the approval of ecclesiastical authorities, who would examine the text for mistakes to avoid "great dangers and errors in the mysteries of the Faith."[24] The increasing scrutiny of texts and suspicion of natives and their "conversion" to the Faith, let alone their translation abilities, led to a drastic decrease in their recognition as assistants and authors by the end of the sixteenth century.

Moreover, such factors combined with the scrutinizing conservatism promoted by the Council of Trent to erode the support for the training of native assistants in schools, such as the College of Tlatelolco, and the production of native-language religious texts. Whereas the eloquence and native rhetoric of many sixteenth- and early seventeenth-century printed texts betray the contributions of native assistants, the increasingly shortened and simplified texts published in the late seventeenth and eighteenth centuries suggest a decline in native-ecclesiastic collaboration. Regardless of such a decline, we may well suspect that oftentimes native assistants continued to work behind the scenes throughout the colonial period to some degree or

21. Sell, "Friars, Nahuas, and Books," 120; Sell, "Classical Age," 28; Bautista, prologue to *Sermonario*, preliminary leaf, unnumbered.

22. Landa, *Relación*, 45, cited in Karttunen, *Between Worlds*, 94. For more on Antonio Chi, see Restall, "Gaspar Antonio Chi."

23. This condition would be modified again by the Second Mexican Provincial Council of 1565. See Lorenzana, *Concilios provinciales*, 201–2.

24. Ibid., 143–44; Sell, "Friars, Nahuas, and Books," 121n20. See also Mosquera, "Nahuatl Catechistic Drama," 58–61.

another. In many cases, a scenario proposed by James Lockhart with regards to the composition of Nahuatl plays likely occurred among other texts, where a Spanish ecclesiastic would write the text in Spanish and then give the text to a native assistant "to translate and realize as he saw fit" without ever looking at it again.[25]

In other cases, natives autonomously created and composed the contents of their own texts. As mentioned, some of the natives trained in the church schools left to become fiscales and maestros in their own towns. Due to their small numbers vis-à-vis the native population, ecclesiastics relied heavily on these indigenous assistants, particularly in Yucatan.[26] The role of fiscales and maestros as surrogate priests granted them a variety of duties that ranged from teaching the doctrine to assisting the dying prepare for death to recording the names of those absent from mass. To assist them in fulfilling such responsibilities, they oftentimes employed Nahuatl and Maya religious texts. Some used printed works; others, although technically forbidden to do so, made their own. When the latter occurred, the doctrinal accuracy of the text depended on the training, interest, and personal preferences of the native author, and this made ecclesiastical authorities nervous.

Although many indigenous authors composed texts that remained within the lines of orthodoxy, others crossed these lines. In recent years scholars have increasingly uncovered native-authored religious texts that represented a form of Christianity that incorporated the natives' preexisting beliefs with those of their European colonizers.[27] Nahua-authored religious plays could alter biblical stories through their adoption of preexisting religious themes, doctrinas could contain heresies, and sermons could take great liberties with Christian doctrine. In a word, in some cases what seemed most important for Nahua and Maya authors was not adhering to doctrinal accuracy

---

25. Lockhart, *Nahuas After the Conquest*, 403.

26. For figures on how many friars were sent to Yucatan and Guatemala-Chiapas, see Early, *Maya and Catholicism*, 134. Early does an excellent job of documenting the important role of maestros today in their communities.

27. For various examples, see Burkhart and Sell, *Nahuatl Theater*; Tavárez, *Invisible War*, 71–73, 129–58; Sánchez de Aguilar, *Informe contra idolorum*, 153–54, 173; and Chuchiak, "Pre-conquest Ah Kinob." More detailed studies of the contributions of Maya maestros and their composition of "forbidden" or "unregulated" literature include Hanks, *Converting Words*, 19, 338–64; Knowlton, *Maya Creation Myths*, 33–51; Bricker and Miram, *Encounter of Two Worlds*; and Christensen, *Nahua and Maya Catholicisms*, 84–88.

but creating a text that conveyed its teachings in ways most familiar and accepted by their native audience. Although ecclesiastics such as Sahagún, fray Diego de Landa, Sánchez de Aguilar, fray Juan Coronel, Hernando Ruiz de Alarcón, Juan Gutiérrez, and many others continued to find and confiscate such texts, they continued in production throughout the colonial period (and beyond!) and contributed to the various Christian messages prescribed and preached.[28]

To be sure, understanding the authors of native-language religious texts assists in understanding the varied content and even orthodoxy of their messages. Yet the texts also provide a better understanding for how Nahua and Maya culture affected the transmission of Christianity. Throughout this book the presentation of Christian doctrine in religious texts betrays their audiences. Divine beings speak in a Nahuatl or Maya rhetoric; the individuals and settings of traditional moralistic stories become localized to central Mexican or Yucatecan surroundings; native epithets and deities are attached to Christian figures. Above all, the worldview of the Nahuas and Mayas continuously influenced the Christian message.[29] Admittedly, such influences are generally more evident in texts produced earlier in the colonial period. Yet all Nahuatl and Maya religious texts translated here, to one degree or another, reflect the culture for which they were intended.

I have attempted to provide a smattering of religious texts that not only represents popular genres but also illustrates their diversity and the range of orthodoxy their messages provided. In exploring these messages, the following examples expose the influence of native and European cultures on the content of the texts themselves. Chapter 1 provides an example of a Nahuatl sermon authored by natives without the direct supervision of ecclesiastical authorities. The sermon is an excellent example of how religiously trained Nahuas could modify ancient Christian legends to accommodate a native audience.

---

28. Burkhart, *Holy Wednesday*, 165; Acuña, "Escritos mayas inéditos," 168–69; Coronel, *Discursos predicables*, xv; Cogolludo, *Historia de Yucatán*, 192–93; Ruiz de Alarcón, *Heathen Superstitions*; Sánchez de Aguilar, *Informe contra idolorum*, 153–54, 173.

29. For some excellent works illustrating the effects of native worldviews on religious texts and evangelization in general, see, for the Nahuas, Burkhart, *Slippery Earth*; for the Mayas, Knowlton, *Maya Creation Myths*; for the Mayas in Guatemala, but also in Chiapas and Yucatan, Early, *Maya and Catholicism*, and Early, *Maya and Catholic Cultures*.

Chapter 2 reveals a similar situation, but for Yucatan through a variety of Maya Christian tales. The remaining three chapters provide examples of common texts and themes: chapter 3 provides translations of a wide variety of texts meant to instruct on the sacrament of baptism, chapter 4 contains Catholic and Methodist catechisms, and chapter 5 deals with confessional manuals. Throughout these chapters the variation among the texts and the diverse messages and concerns they betray become evident to illustrate the rich and assorted instruction available to natives through the translated Christianities of Nahuatl and Maya religious texts.

1

Saint Paul and Saint Sebastian in the "Nahuatl Bible"

We (Nahua nobles) no longer believe and still we will love those you (Spaniards) do
not yet take to be gods; still before our gods we will kill people; it will again be like it
was before you came here.
—"Nahuatl Bible," before 1560

Religiously trained Nahuas and Mayas composed religious texts
under varying degrees of ecclesiastic supervision. A small manuscript
cataloged in the Schøyen Collection as "The Nahuatl Bible" provides
an excellent example of a Nahua-authored religious text that received
virtually no oversight from religious authorities. The anonymous
text is a sermon recounting a Nahua version of the conversion of
Saint Paul and the ministry of Saint Sebastian and dates to sometime before 1560. The manuscript itself spans eight folios, or sixteen
pages, and has two vellum sheets sewn on either side that serve as
its cover. Interestingly, the manuscript contains sixty-four profiles
of Nahua heads on the front pastedown, which is made of *amatl*,
or fig-tree bark paper (see fig. 1). Over the years various scholars
have proposed diverse explanations for the heads that range from
tributaries to actors in a play. Yet when composing manuscript works,
authors sometimes employed pieces of heavier paper to make covers.[1]
Thus, it is possible, and even likely, that the heads correspond with a
separate work altogether and not the sermon. The manuscript fails to
reveal its origins, and today resides in Europe as part of the Schøyen
Collection, MS 1692.[2]

---

1. An excellent example would be the 1713 manuscript of Joseph Antonio Pérez
de la Fuente's manuscript "Relación mercurina," no. 10, Department of Rare Books
and Special Collections, Garrett Collection of Mesoamerican Manuscripts (C0744),
Princeton University Library.

2. The manuscript is mentioned in Gómez de Orozco, *Catálogo*, 157–58; Glass,
"Census," 175; and Horcasitas, *Teatro náhuatl*, 447–59, 601–3, which includes a tran-
scription and loose Spanish translation of the text by Faustino Galicia Chimalpopoca.
My transcription, however, varies from that found in Horcasitas's work.

Fig. 1 Inside cover and first page of the "Nahuatl Bible." MS 1692, Schøyen Collection. Courtesy of the Schøyen Collection, Oslo.

A variety of evidence exists to confidently suggest the Nahua authorship of the sermon. First and foremost, the sermon contains numerous deviances regarding the history and lives of Saint Paul and Saint Sebastian—deviances that a priest would never have allowed knowingly. In the Bible, Paul was once Saul, a Pharisee who zealously persecuted Christians in the first century and even witnessed the stoning of the prophet Stephen. When traveling to Damascus on a mission to arrest Christians, "suddenly there shined round about him a light from heaven, and he fell to the earth, and heard a voice saying unto him, 'Saul, Saul, why persecutest thou me?' And he said, 'Who art thou, Lord?' And the Lord said, 'I am Jesus whom thou persecutest.'" The encounter caused Saul to lose his sight until his companions took him to Damascus, where the Christian, Ananias, blessed him. Saul then became baptized and began a lifelong ministry preaching of Christ. The moment at which Saul adopted the name Paul is unclear, but it was not at his baptism.[3]

Adding to the biblical history of Paul is the *Vision of Saint Paul*, which relates Paul's visit to heaven and hell in a vision to witness the rewards of the righteous and the punishment of the damned.

3. Acts 9:3–5, 10 (AV). Not until Acts 13:9 is Saul referred to as Paul.

Reportedly, versions of the text first appeared in Latin Antiquity in Greek, then in Latin; subsequent renditions in the vernacular then emerged throughout Western Europe. Dante even references Paul's vision in his fourteenth-century *Divine Comedy*.[4] Although various religious authorities expressed their doubts as to its doctrinal validity, the tale was popular and very influential during the Middle Ages, and many of the friars who trained the Nahuas in religion and writing certainly would have been familiar with its contents.[5] That the friars used such tales to instruct the Nahuas is very likely, especially when considering that similar medieval stories were used to educate the Yucatec Mayas (see chapter 2).

Our knowledge of Saint Sebastian derives not from the Bible but from later hagiographies (biographies of saints and religious leaders) and texts that became popular in the Middle Ages, such as Jacobus de Voragine's *The Golden Legend* (ca. 1260). At the time of the arrival of the Spaniards in Mexico, *The Golden Legend* was available in Spanish as the *Flos sanctorum*. According to these works, Sebastian died as a Christian martyr in 287 A.D. at the orders of the Roman emperor Diocletian and, subsequently, at the hands of Roman soldiers who shot him with arrows. After Sebastian miraculously survived the arrows and reprimanded Diocletian, the emperor ordered Sebastian beaten to death and his body thrown in a sewer.[6]

The Nahuatl sermon, which itself resembles a hagiography, alters nearly every part of these two accounts (see tables 1 and 2).[7] The religious training of the Nahua author(s) surely provided a familiarity with Saint Paul and Saint Sebastian. Fray Bernardino de Sahagún's *Psalmodia christiana* (1583) describes the life of Sebastian in some detail.[8] Moreover, the *Flos sanctorum* was a "best seller" of sorts and commonplace among the libraries of ecclesiastics and the laity

---

4. See, for example, Dante, *Inferno*, canto 2, line 32.

5. For more of a comparison of the Nahuatl and medieval tale, see Christensen, *Nahua and Maya Catholicisms*, 199. Silverstein provides an excellent study of the text in his *Visio Sancti Pauli*. See also Sautman, Conchado, and Di Scipio, *Telling Tales*, 109–10. The act of God showing a sinner the pains of hell to inspire repentance was a common theme in many European didactic tales throughout the Middle Ages (see chapter 2). For a few examples, see Gayangos, *Escritores*, 478–79.

6. *Flos sanctorum*, fols. 40r–42r; Jacobus, *Golden Legend*, 50–54.

7. Morgan explains the close and symbiotic relationship between sermons and hagiographies in his *Spanish American Saints*, 35–36.

8. Sahagún, *Psalmodia christiana*, 47–51.

Table 1 Comparison of the biblical and Nahua accounts of the conversion of Paul

Biblical account
Saul holds the cloaks of those who stone the prophet Stephen
Saul loses his sight
Saul goes to Damascus to restore his sight
Saul is baptized and learns the Christian doctrine
Saul begins to be referred to as Paul

Nahua account
Paul and his followers shoot Sebastian with arrows
Paul is turned to dust
Paul goes to heaven to converse with God
Paul goes to hell
Paul's body miraculously regains its form
Paul and his followers retrieve Sebastian and take him to Paul's home
Paul burns his idols
Peter comes to Paul's home to baptize and instruct him in reading and writing
Peter changes Paul's name to Pablo

Sources: Acts 9–10 (AV); "Nahuatl Bible," MS 1692, Schøyen Collection, 1–9. Table adapted from Christensen, "Tales of Two Cultures," 370. Used with permission.

of central Mexico.[9] Yet the Nahua author(s) alter various elements of the individual story lines. For example, in the sermon Paul and his followers kill Sebastian with arrows; an event strangely familiar with Paul witnessing the stoning of Stephen. And whereas the *Vision of Saint Paul* recounts a vision awarded to a converted Paul for his righteousness, in the Nahuatl sermon Paul is a sinner who not only witnesses the torments of hell but also is a victim of them.

In other instances, the Nahuatl sermon adds elements to the story lines to serve its own didactic agenda—in this case, the cessation of idolatry and the promotion of Christian virtues. As a result, Paul the Pharisee becomes an idolater who tries to kill Sebastian, is turned to dust, goes to heaven and hell, miraculously regains his body, burns his idols, and is baptized by Peter. On the other hand,

---

9. Fernández del Castillo, *Libros y libreros*, 55, 264–81; Nesvig, *Ideology and Inquisition*, 237–41; Mathes, *First Academic Library*, 4–5. Interestingly, the Inquisition banned the 1558 edition printed in Zaragoza.

Table 2 Comparison of the *Flos sanctorum* and the Nahua sermon on the ministry of Sebastian

Flos sanctorum
Sebastian is a clandestine Christian in the Praetorian Guard
Sebastian performs covert works of charity
Sebastian converts a variety of people, including the prefect of Rome
Diocletian discovers Sebastian is a Christian and orders his execution by arrows
Sebastian survives
Sebastian harangues Diocletian
Diocletian orders Sebastian beaten to death

Nahua account
Paul kills Sebastian, who is miraculously brought back to life
Sebastian preaches in an altepetl
Sebastian chastises the Nahua nobility for their common practices
The nobles disregard Sebastian and revert to their ways of idolatry
Sebastian is cast out of the altepetl
Sebastian desires to be punished in hell
God himself speaks to Sebastian, offering comfort and encouragement to try again

Sources: *Flos sanctorum*, 40r–42r; "Nahuatl Bible," MS 1692, Schøyen Collection, 9–16. Table adapted from Christensen, "Nahuatl in Evangelization," 701. Used with permission.

Sebastian—whose role of sweeping the roads to heaven parallels Nahua culture, where precontact priests regularly swept the temples of their gods—is shot by Paul with arrows and subsequently preaches repentance to nobles with strong Nahua characteristics. Above all, the Nahuatl text transports, however figuratively, these two prophets to the Americas, where they speak, dress, and behave like—and, for all intents and purposes, become—Nahuas.

The early date of the sermon and its goal to reform the Nahuas, particularly the nobility, remind us of the concerted effort among ecclesiastics in the 1530s to reform many of the baptized Nahua nobility who continued to practice precontact traditions that conflicted with Christianity—specifically polygamy, idolatry, and avaricious living. Trained Nahua youth were often the messengers of such reform, and certain Nahuas, such as don Carlos Ometochtli, scoffed at the audaciousness of such young boys in instructing them to relinquish their idolatry and polygamy.[10] Although the assertion is speculative, it is tempting to consider this sermon as reflective of the messages these young religious assistants brought to the ears of the Nahua nobility.

The Nahua authorship and influence of the text also emerges in its native rhetoric and misspelling of common Spanish words (such as "diaplos" or "tiablos" for *diablos*). Interestingly, the orthography and penmanship of the sermon indicates that two individual Nahua hands wrote the script, suggesting that the sermon we have today is a copy of a separate Nahua-authored manuscript.[11] Regardless, the Nahuatl sermon itself represents an excellent example of those texts ecclesiastical authorities would surely have confiscated had they known about them or their contents. Here, it seems the goal of the Nahua author(s) was not to replicate a doctrinally accurate account of the conversion of Saint Paul or the ministry of Saint Sebastian but rather to use these figures in didactic stories that aligned more evenly with Nahua culture. Whether written for use in the convents and local schools to train other Nahuas, or as a Sunday sermon, the result is a wonderful example of how Nahuatl religious texts could familiarize Christian doctrine and contain very unorthodox material.

The "Nahuatl Bible" (before 1560), 1–16

Then, along with the others, Paul's horse was running; our lord God brought about that his horse was struck by lightning. And then Paul's body quickly crumbled greatly and all turned to dust. His demons just gathered it up and put it in a cloak. And then Paul went straight to heaven.

And when our lord God saw Paul, he said to him, "Why did you kill Sebastian, for he builds temples for me and sweeps on the

10. Don, *Bonfires of Culture*, 167, 89. For more on the Franciscan's morals campaign, see ibid., 146–74, and Gruzinski, *Man-Gods*, 31–62.

11. Philologically and orthographically the manuscript points to distinct preferences among the native writers. Both writers tend to use abbreviations incorrectly and interchange the *u* and the *n* throughout. The first writer is prone to omit syllables, which sometimes he catches and writes in. Also confirming the early date of the text is its occasional use of the *huehuetlatolli* form of rhetoric in a phrase for "thank you." My thanks to James Lockhart for his insights.

road by which they enter my home in heaven? I am merciful to my children, the poor or humble who are afflicted, who endure hardships and earn their way with effort. I am not merciful to those who have possessions, belongings, and many houses but to those without houses on earth who greatly suffer.

"Now, Paul, really look where the humble come to settle. I am caring for the happiness, prosperity, riches of those who cry, are sad, sigh, who always go about seeking me, languishing greatly, joining their hands, who kneel down. This heaven will be the house of them only; here are their houses, houses of gold; they will come to sit on golden seats, for no one else sits on their seats. And now that you have beheld it, Paul, can you count all that is here, the eternal happiness and prosperity? And now that you have seen it, look also at hell, for there is much fire and smoke there, and the smoke reeks badly. My children the angels will go along, taking care of you."

Then the angels took him to hell. And Paul saw things in hell; he was very frightened and wept; he stood on the hot coals for only a short time, but it seemed to him like twenty years. He saw the semblance of the devils and demons with their iron tongs with which they cut us up; they place our bodies in metal tubs; the evil ones never give relief in all eternity. Paul saw and beheld a great deal; all the torments cannot be expressed, cannot all be told, we cannot mention them all here. And when Paul came to, he greatly wept and was very sad.

The angels told Paul, "Be afraid, look upon the evil demons with fear! Serve them no longer, no longer make offerings to them, get rid of those whom you served and venerated as gods, before whom you bled yourself and also before whom you were cutting your ears, the evil demons."

And when he had regained consciousness, three times he said, "Jesus, Jesus, Jesus."

Then all those who were there, who had been keeping his body, said, "Is the ruler (Paul) a bad omen for us? And how is it that his body was collected and we gathered it up in bits?"

But Paul told them, "Don't take me for something monstrous, my lords, let me loose. As to what I saw and beheld, now I will speak to you and tell you what I beheld; for we sinned greatly when we killed God's beloved, such a thing should not have been done. Go and bring back Sebastian's body; because of this I had died. But now our lord God still favors me."

Then, they went to get Sebastian from where they had repeatedly shot arrows at him. And when they went and got Sebastian, from very far away there could be seen his light that our lord God in heaven placed upon him (Sebastian). Then they loosened his body; it was still as though he had not died; he was still very sound; the reason he was very sound was that the angels of God helped him; they brought him to Paul's home.

Then he (Paul) said, "O my honored noble, greetings; I went to heaven and saw our lord God, and I also went to see things in hell. It was on your behalf that I went to behold things. And now, let the evil devils that are in my home be burned." This is what Paul said.

They then removed those (idols) they had taken to be gods and cast them down in the patio and there they burned and scorched them. And when they had burned, Paul told Sebastian, "O my honored noble, Sebastian, since the devils have been burned, for your sake baptize me."

Then, he (Sebastian) told him, "It is not I who is to baptize you; a person will baptize you who lives very far away; let them go call him; his name is Peter."

When he had come, Paul related to him how it was when he went to see heaven and hell. Then Peter baptized Paul and he (Peter) changed his name; he baptized and called him Paul. After he had baptized him, he taught him reading and writing. It did not take a whole day to teach him, but just a short time. By midday, he could already write; he wrote everything having to do with prayer and holy examples, and everything about how we people of the earth, we humans, are to live respectfully.

And in addition, we all will earnestly pray to our father Saint Paul. The reason that we will earnestly pray to him is that he believed afterward, and with us too it was after we believed that we burned the evil demons we had taken to be gods. We are not alone or the only ones who have done it this way; for our father Saint Paul did it the same way, for which reason we will earnestly pray on his feast day to our lord. Also, he (Paul) will pray to our lord God for us; that is all of the statement; it is to be observed well.

The story of the life of God's beloved, named Sebastian, who was truly a very great preacher and servant of our savior and lord Jesus Christ; he was a true child of God. Sebastian was preaching in an *altepetl;*[12] he was revealing his message and commandments; he was spreading the message and orders that the Christians called his commandments, the divine orders of God. And Sebastian was preaching to the people and very truly they had known and been inspired by the sermon; they saw and understood a very great deal of the divine words that Sebastian showed them and made known to them.

When his pupils had learned much of the divine words, Sebastian then assembled all the rulers, nobles, and all the commoners. He told them, "Come all of you, you rulers and nobles." Then he said, "You heard and understood God's word as I told it to you; not only is it said that God will have mercy on us in heaven, but we will do many things so that he will be very merciful to us and very happy with us now. Listen you rulers and nobles! God does not want you to have many women (wives) or many slaves. Today, that is all with which I do my duty toward you so that God can favor you. Cast out your women and your slaves and all your home dwellers! May they leave! And as to your houses, grant them to those who have no house, give them to the poor. And your gold/silver, all your property, your cloaks, and all that is in your home, give it all away, and also your fields. And all those who serve you whom you greatly mistreat, who produce for you what you need, whom you greatly mistreat, our lord God does not want it so."

And after he (Sebastian) had told them this, they became angry about it; thereupon they (the nobles) said, "What are you saying to us Sebastian? It is bad. When we were baptized, you told us, 'Because of it God will have mercy on you.' And after we were baptized, now you tell us, 'Get rid of your wives; give all your property, all that is in your homes and your houses, to those without houses, all those who are poor.' After we give it to them, where will we go, for we will no longer have property? In what will we appear as rulers when we have served the poor? And now we do not want this to be done; we had really believed your words, but now we no longer believe; we abandon what you had taught us; we no longer believe and still we will love those you do not yet take to be gods; still before our gods we will kill people; it will again be like it was before you came here."

After the wicked had said this to Sebastian, God's beloved was very sad and wept. He told them, "Listen evildoers! What are

12. Nahua municipal community or town.

you saying? Is it not a sin that you want to break our lord God's commandments?"

But the wicked no longer listened at all to him at that point; still he tried to restrain them, but they said, "Although it is sin, did we ask you about it? We really no longer want what you tell us; we no longer want you to live here. Go to your home, to where you came from."

When they had said this, then Sebastian kneeled and joined his hands and prayed to our lord God; when he prayed to him, he said, O *elluhe. dīē*,[13] O God, O Giver of Life,[14] how can it be that wretched I behaved inconsiderately toward you and offended you and did not do my duty with your holy commands so that people were not able to retain what they were taught? Have me burned, may I see the torments of hell. As for the people, may you be merciful with them O lord."

Then our lord God himself replied to him and said to him in turn, "O Sebastian, weep no longer, no longer be so sad. I saw the wicked, you did not sin; you redeemed yourself, you did your duty. They broke my commandments on their own. . . . Try them again![15] Never . . . was in vain . . . when no longer they consent, you are to tell me again."

After our lord had declared this to him, then . . . replied . . . Sebastian told him . . . , "Thank you, let me try them out again."

Then, he goes to try them; when he reached the people he said to them, "Listen you people! You say you really do not love the words, the commandments of our lord God. Today I came at his bidding; maybe I will try you out another time. May you judge it well!"

13. Unknown epithet.
14. *Ipalnemohuani*. This is an epithet for Nahua creator deities such as Tezcatlipoca and even Quetzalcoatl.
15. Here and in a few other places the manuscript has been damaged by water, rendering a transcription and translation of certain words difficult, if not impossible.

2

Maya Christian Tales

All these things spake Jesus unto the multitude in parables; and without a parable
spake he not unto them.
—Matthew 13:34

As seen in the previous chapter, religious texts employed stories,
however unorthodox, to convey their messages. The short story
is perhaps the most enduring and popular genre of didactic literature throughout time. Aesop, Chaucer, Dickens, Shakespeare,
and the Brothers Grimm all understood the value of an engaging
tale—whether fictitious or factual—to convey a message or simply to entertain. The efficacy of the short story to educate was not
lost on Christianity. Indeed, in the New Testament, Christ himself
mastered the genre with his use of parables intended to inspire and
instruct. Throughout the Middle Ages, the short story and hagiography genres blended nearly seamlessly in various European works
such as Saint Gregory's *Dialogues* (590s) and Jacobus de Voragine's
The Golden Legend (ca. 1260).[1] Other medieval works, including Clemente Sánchez de Vercial's early fifteenth-century *The Book of Tales
by A. B. C.* and later editions of *History of the Maiden Teodora*,
also employed short stories to convey Christian morals.[2] Furthermore, illustrative stories, or exempla, in religious texts, particularly
sermons, were designed to provide contemporary examples of ancient
doctrine.[3] Spaniards embraced the genre, and numerous works
appeared in the vernacular.[4]

Many of these manuscripts saw print throughout the early modern period and influenced the Spanish ecclesiastics who would carry

1. Today, modern readers have easy access to these works. See Saint Gregory,
Dialogues, and Jacobus, *Golden Legend.*
2. Sánchez de Vercial, *Book of Tales;* Parker, *Story of a Story.*
3. For more on exempla, and particularly the sermon exempla, see Scanlon, *Narrative, Authority, and Power,* 27–36, 57–80.
4. Maire Bobes, *Cuentos,* 23–36.

such works across the Atlantic to the Americas.[5] Here, in some form or another, the dialogues of Saint Gregory, the legends of Jacobus, the tales of Sánchez, and the popular stories of the maiden Teodora and Emperor Hadrian would find their way into the Yucatecan schools established to train the sons of the Maya nobility in reading, writing, and religion. As a result of their exposure to these stories, Maya authors occasionally included them in their works.[6] The Maya stories translated here provide examples of this occurrence.

The following stories derive from a Maya manuscript of unknown authorship and origin commonly referred to as the Morley Manuscript. The date 1576 is located within the manuscript's pages and much of the text does seem to originate in the early colonial period.[7] Centuries later Sylvanus Morley would acquire the manuscript and bequeath it to the Museum of Indian Arts and Culture in Santa Fe, New Mexico. Gretchen Whalen's recent transcription and translation of the text has pulled the manuscript out of relative obscurity and opened the door for further insights into early colonial Yucatec Maya writing. Whalen suggests that the text, and its rhetoric, orthography, and content, betrays its author as a Maya maestro serving as a

5. Perhaps the most common of these among private and ecclesiastical libraries in Spain was Jacobus's work, which, as was mentioned, was translated into Spanish as the *Flos sanctorum*. See Pettas, *Sixteenth-Century Spanish Bookstore*, 72, 122, 159.

6. For example, Whalen notes that portions of the Morley Manuscript, not covered here, derived from *Las preguntas que el emperador hizo al infante Epitus*, a 1540 publication banned by the Inquisition in 1559. See her "Annotated Translation." Stories similar to those addressed here also appear in the Maya-authored Chilam Balam of Tusik. Furthermore, the story of the maiden Teodora appears in the Chilam Balams of Chan Kan, Kaua, Ixil, and the Códice Pérez. See Parker, *Story of a Story*, 11–13; George-Hirons, "Tell Me, Maiden"; and Bricker and Miram, *Encounter of Two Worlds*, 33–36. As we have seen, ecclesiastics and Nahuas similarly employed medieval stories in their texts. For a particularly illustrative example, see Burkhart, "Voyage of Saint Amaro." Justyna Olko-Bajer uncovered a sixteenth-century Nahuatl manuscript (Codex Indianorum 7) in the John Carter Brown Library, relating an account of Judas that also appears in *The Golden Legend* and *Flos sanctorum* in their discussions of Saint Matthias. Furthermore, the works of Clemente Sánchez de Vercial and Johannes Gobius influenced Nahuatl texts on Mary; see Burkhart, "'Here Is Another Marvel,'" and Burkhart, *Before Guadalupe*, 5, 133–34. European playwrights Lope de Vega Carpio and Pedro Calderón de la Barca inspired Nahuatl plays; see Wright, "Dramatic Diaspora." For other examples of European texts and their Nahuatl counterparts, see Burkhart, *Holy Wednesday*, and Kutscher, Brotherston, and Vollmer, *Aesop in Mexico*.

7. The existing manuscript appears to date to the late eighteenth century; these texts were commonly recopied and amended over the years. For additional details on dating the text, see Whalen, "Annotated Translation," and Knowlton, "Dynamics."

schoolmaster who frequently refers to his audience as "young men."[8] Thus, although the intentions of the text revolved around the evangelization of its audience, the manuscript and autonomous nature of the text itself renders it technically unofficial and forbidden.

The manuscript contains a variety of writings on Christian subjects, including a series of short stories, six of which are included here. In her initial analysis of the manuscript, Whalen noted that some of its short stories were biblical, while others appeared in the texts of Jacobus and Sánchez.[9] After further searching, I succeeded in connecting each of the six stories to either a biblical account or a story found in the earlier works of Jacobus, Sánchez, Saint Gregory, Jacques de Vitry, and others. The shortened, abbreviated nature of the stories in the Morley Manuscript compared to their medieval or biblical counterparts suggests that their original Maya author either composed them from memory or took great liberty with their redactions instead of providing a direct translation from text. To illustrate the influence of Maya culture on the tales, I include some brief commentary at the beginning of each of the six stories, comparing the Yucatec Maya version of the tale to its medieval or biblical counterpart.

All the stories found in the Morley Manuscript cover topics and themes relevant to the Maya Christians of colonial Yucatan. In addition to the overarching theme of living a true Christian lifestyle, the tales translated here speak to the specific topics of chastity, the supreme power of God, testaments, idolatry, confession, and the punishment of the wicked in purgatory and hell—themes that appeared repeatedly in religious texts throughout the colonial period. In fact, many of the sections found within the Morley Manuscript also appear in other Maya works, both unpublished and published. The Books of Chilam Balam—Maya-authored manuscripts containing a variety of topics pertaining to Maya culture and history—from the towns of Kaua and Chan Kan both contain sections similar to those found in the Morley Manuscript, and some sections of fray

---

8. Whalen, "Annotated Translation." For additional analysis on the manuscript, see Christensen, *Nahua and Maya Catholicisms*, 201–3; Knowlton, "Dynamics"; and Knowlton, *Maya Creation Myths*, 48–51. I owe a large debt of gratitude to the initial legwork performed by Whalen on the Morley Manuscript.

9. Whalen, "Annotated Translation."

Juan Coronel's 1620 *Discursos predicables* follow the manuscript nearly word for word, including some of the stories translated here.[10]

Writing in a style similar to the composition of European exempla, Maya authors frequently engaged in a kind of "text sharing/borrowing." For example, cognate versions of a redaction of the creation of the world, or "Genesis Commentary," can be found in the Chilam Balams of Kaua and Chan Kan, the Morley Manuscript, and in a newly discovered manuscript from Teabo.[11] These instances of borrowing among Maya texts should not be considered plagiarism by modern standards. Instead, the borrowing of stories was commonplace in both New Spain and Europe, as many authors borrowed from one another's work to produce similar tales.[12] In general, it is clear that genres popular to the Mayas—such as these didactic stories or the "Genesis Commentary"—were widely circulated among the unofficial texts of the Mayas.

Overall, the Morley Manuscript and its short stories are an important link in a chain connecting didactic religious stories from the initial centuries of Christianity in Europe to the colonial period in the Americas. Indeed, it is incredible to consider that these short stories—some of which date back to at least the fourth century—made their way across the European continent and the Atlantic to appear in colonial Maya texts located in small native towns in remote Yucatan! Although such tales no doubt continued in oral tradition, their appearance on paper diminished beginning in the seventeenth century, as ecclesiastics increasingly became wary of the "superstitious" and "unorthodox" material these stories contained.[13] As far as I can tell, such stories in Yucatec Maya last appeared, at least in official printed works, in Coronel's 1620 *Discursos predicables*, although some continued in unofficial manuscripts well beyond the colonial period.

10. Many of the Chilam Balams included doctrinal material. For some excellent studies on the matter, see Bricker and Miram, *Encounter of Two Worlds*; Hanks, *Converting Words*; Knowlton, *Maya Creation Myths*; Knowlton, "Dynamics"; and Caso Barrera, *Chilam Balam de Ixil*.

11. I recently discovered a manuscript while searching in the archives of Brigham Young University that appears to be a Maya Christian copybook from Teabo. For more on the manuscript and its contents, see "Teabo Manuscript."

12. Sánchez de Vercial, *Book of Tales*, 2–6.

13. For more on the censorship of early Mexican texts, see Nesvig, *Ideology and Inquisition*.

Saint Justina

This first story is a love story of sorts. It tells of a man, Cyprian, who in his desperate attempts to be with the virgin Justina requests the assistance of the devil. But despite his attempts the devil has no power over Justina because of her "true Christianity." Seeing the superior power of the righteous over the devil, Cyprian converts to Christianity. The story ends by instructing the Maya audience that "true" or worthy Christians need not fear devils or their temptations.

The story of Cyprian and Justina also appears in Jacobus's *The Golden Legend* and its Spanish translation in the *Flos sanctorum*.[14] Yet there are differences. Generally speaking, the Maya story is a shortened, somewhat diluted version of that found in Jacobus's medieval text. For example, Jacobus includes many more details on the various attempts of the devil and his minions to ensnare Justina. During these attempts, the European tale repeatedly emphasizes the power of the sign of the cross in repelling the devil, whereas the Maya text simply ascribes Justina's superior power to her "true Christianity." This concept of the benefits gained by living a Christian lifestyle is one seen repeatedly throughout religious texts intended for the Mayas and reflects an overall concern for Maya converts who only partially subscribed to their Christian religion. In addition, *The Golden Legend* and the *Flos sanctorum* identify Justina as the daughter of a pagan who converts to Christianity. The Maya version omits mentioning this conversion and confusingly describes Justina as both a *ma ocolal*, "nonbeliever," and *u palil Dios*, "a servant of God." This lack of clarity could make the audience wonder with some confusion as to why the pagan Justina was a true Christian with power over the devil.

EXCERPT FROM THE MORLEY MANUSCRIPT, 325–27

*The Devil Does Not Conquer Except for He Who
Desires to Allow Himself to Be Conquered*
There was a female and a male nonbeliever in another town.[15] His name was Cyprian. Well, because he lusted for a virgin, a servant of

---

14. Jacobus, *Golden Legend*, 243–47; *Flos sanctorum*, fols. 212r–213v.
15. All subheadings occur in the original manuscript. For all translations from the Morley Manuscript, I use Whalen's transcription, modifying spacing and orthography

God whose name was Justina, when Cyprian saw that he was unable to deceive the woman, nor subdue the virgin, he invoked the devil to help him.

He said to him, "Know that I really lust for the woman Justina, nor am I able to complete it so that I deceive her; therefore, go deceive her for me, so she submits to me."

Then the devil went to strive to deceive the servant of God (Justina), but he was not able to either. So then the devil said to Cyprian, "Know that Justina is unable to be deceived because of her true Christianity. I cannot corrupt true Christians. If perhaps their Christianity is feigned, they could be tempted by me, but the power against good Christians is insufficient," stated the devil.

Then Cyprian began to consider this; this then was the reason he began to despise the devil while he entered into the service of God.

Therefore, if your Christianity is true, you young man, what do you have to fear of devils and their deceiving you, because the power against you is insufficient?[16]

The Negligent Executor

In this story the audience is told of a Maya warrior whose last will and testament instructs his friend to sell his horses to settle his debts. After the warrior died, the friend kept the horses for his own instead of selling them. Eventually the warrior appears to his friend and relates the suffering he endured in purgatory because of his unsettled debts. The warrior warns his friend that he will die an unpleasant death due to his failure to sell the horses. Sure enough, a few days later the friend "died while being ripped apart by jaguars and wild animals."[17]

Sánchez's *The Book of Tales by A. B. C.* contains a very similar account with the same basic story line. Yet again there are

---

to my own personal preference. As mentioned, Whalen's report to FAMSI includes an English translation of the stories. Although our translations convey a similar account, they differ nevertheless due to personal preferences and interpretations of the text itself. That said, I owe a large debt of gratitude to Whalen for her pioneering translation.

16. The story is also found in Coronel, *Discursos predicables*, fols. 191v–192r.

17. Morley Manuscript, 329–30, as appears in Whalen, "Annotated Translation."

differences. Instead of a Maya warrior, Sánchez's tale has a knight; instead of dying from jaguars and wild animals, devils, "sounding just like wolves and lions," snatch the knight's entrusted, who is found twelve days later atop a willow tree, four days' journey from the city.[18] Additionally, whereas the Maya version speaks of selling the horses to settle debts, Sánchez's knight wants the money donated to benefit the poor, and thus his soul.

Understanding that warriors and jaguars were familiar subjects in Maya culture, the differences between the European and Maya stories arguably derive from the author's modifications of the story to fit a Maya audience. Yet it remains unclear why the Maya author chose to have the warrior's final request refer to his debts rather than a specific offering for his posthumous soul or even charity. Certainly, the necessity of settling everyday debts was ever present among the colonial Mayas, and it even appeared in their last wills and testaments.[19] But the importance of praying and doing works for those in purgatory was also understood by the Mayas, and testators frequently set aside funds in their wills to provide postmortem aid to their souls in purgatory. Among the Mayas in Yucatan, the most common bequest was an offering of money, or even material goods, to pay for a requiem mass for their souls. In 1646 Juana Mukul from the Maya town of Cacalchen designated three *tostones*, or twelve *reales*, for her mass, and in 1654 Andrés Uitz, from the same town, ordered the sale of his possessions to cover the fee.[20] Ecclesiastics also instructed the Mayas to give charitable alms to the "Jerusalem fund." Originally established to support the Christian Crusades, the fund operated in colonial Yucatan as a sinecure and even as a part of the local ecclesiastic's income. In his 1647 will Bonaventura Canche donated twelve candles, two measures of maize, four chickens, and two *tomines* for "the work in Jerusalem."[21]

Whether leaving money for debts or the posthumous care of their souls, Maya testators appointed executors to ensure the completion

18. Sánchez de Vercial, *Book of Tales*, 200. Jacques de Vitry also includes this story in his earlier *Exempla*, but the negligent executor is carried in the air by a flock of black crows that drop him on a stone, breaking his neck (183).

19. See Restall, *Life and Death*, 124–26; and Restall, *Maya World*, 183.

20. Eight reales equaled one peso. Christensen, *Nahua and Maya Catholicisms*, 277–78.

21. Ibid., 278. A tomín is a coin, weight, or standard of value. One tomín is equivalent to one real.

of such bequests. The 1766 will of Nicolasa Tec of Ixil stated, "I now appoint one nobleman, Andres Cob, as executor; he shall take care to request a mass (for my soul)."[22] Ecclesiastics warned natives about the consequences of not fulfilling their responsibilities as executors. The topic was even the theme of a play written in Nahuatl that instructed its audience on the horrible fate that awaits those who do not honor the wishes of testators.[23] In this Maya story we see a similar attempt to convey the importance of fulfilling the final desires of the testator, in this case, the settling of debts.

EXCERPT FROM THE MORLEY MANUSCRIPT, 329–30

How God Punishes Those Who Do Not Fulfill Testaments
It was written in the book of the works of the saints in this way: when death had come to a warrior,[24] he commended his order (will) to a friend. Then he said to him, "This must be, friend. I am leaving horses to you which, when I die, you will sell, and give the payment to those with whom I have a debt."

Then his friend said, "It will be, lord. I will complete your order."

Then the warrior died, but the friend did not want to sell the horses and pay the warrior's debt; instead he had taken the horses for himself because they appeared good to him.

After a few days the warrior manifested himself to his friend; he said, "Woe to you, you who impedes orders, for the great evil you did to me, nor was the suffering small that I passed through in the torments of purgatory because you failed to pay my debt. But having finally completed my penance, I am going to rejoice with God; but you, you are about to die, and the end of your life will not be good because you took for yourself my horses, and you failed to complete my order that I gave to you."

The warrior then left, there was no impediment or delay in the fulfillment of his words about his friend, for he died very suddenly while being torn apart by jaguars and wild animals.

22. Restall, *Life and Death*, 69.
23. Sell and Burkhart, *Death and Life*, 165–89.
24. Here the Maya word is *hoolcane*. Holkan literally means "head of the serpent," and it referred to those warriors who served under the chief Maya military captain and who were paid only during military campaigns by both the captain and the *cah*, or Maya town.

You see the manner of the penance for not desiring to complete the order and the last will and testament of the dying?[25]

The Pains of Purgatory

This tale instructs on the pains of purgatory. In the Maya tale the protagonist is a sick man who suffered greatly from his illness. While he pleads with God for death, an angel appears and tells him that he has not completely repented of his sins. But the angel offers him a choice: one year of suffering from the illness or one day in purgatory. The afflicted chooses purgatory, to whence his soul is immediately sent. After he thought many *katuns* had passed—a katun is a unit of time in the Maya calendar that equals 7,200 days, or nearly twenty years—he asked the angel why he had tricked him. The angel replied that he had been in purgatory only a few moments, as his dead body on earth was still warm. He then chose to return to his body and live out his one year of illness.

As we saw in chapter 1 with the *Vision of Saint Paul,* European stories popular throughout the Middle Ages and beyond that allowed sinners to glimpse the horrors of hell could influence native works. Here is yet another example. Various texts attribute this story to Saint Anthony.[26] Jacques de Vitry's exempla also contain a similar tale, recounting a sick man given the option of a long illness or two days in purgatory.[27] Moreover, *The Golden Legend* contains a comparable account of Saint Gregory, who chose a lifetime of pain and sickness over two days in purgatory.[28] The Maya and European accounts are generally similar and even agree on the detail of the dead body still lying warm in its bed. The primary difference is a cultural one and involves the use of Maya calendrical units to describe the perceived time passed in purgatory. Interestingly, most European versions of the story place the perceived time in purgatory as "several" or sometimes

---

25. This story also appears in Coronel, *Discursos predicables,* fols. 194v–195r.

26. See, for example, M. Ricard, *Twelve Months,* 33–34.

27. Jacques de Vitry, *Exempla,* cvi. For an excellent discussion of exempla in Spain and for more on Jacques de Vitry's contributions and connections to these Spanish texts, see ciii–cvi. The story also appears in Étienne de Besançon's thirteenth-century *Alphabet of Tales,* 441–42. Other manuscripts citing the story can be found in Tubach, *Index Exemplorum,* 307.

28. Jacobus, *Golden Legend,* 99.

even "many" years. The Maya account assigns "many katuns"; even if we were to take this to mean only, say, five katuns (or roughly one hundred years), it makes for quite a dramatic example.

EXCERPT FROM THE MORLEY MANUSCRIPT, 331–33

How the Pains of Purgatory Are Great

A servant of God was being greatly afflicted when his body began to grow painful, and when his torment seemed to him unbearable he begged God to leave this earth in order to end his torment. That was his desire.

Then an angel said, "See, understand that you have not finished appeasing God regarding your sin. Because of this, choose any of the two you desire: if you desire to reside in your bed in your torment for one year, then you remain. But if you desire to go to the suffering of purgatory for one day, then you will go."

The sick person said, "I desire more to go to the suffering of purgatory for one day because one whole day passes quickly," he says.

Then the sick person died; he went to the suffering of purgatory for one day, then he began to be greatly afflicted with really grave torments. Shortly after his torments had barely begun, he said to the angel, "Oh, my misery! How could you allow me this, you who are an angel? Did you not say to me that I will be placed here for truly one day? Then how did the time of my suffering become extended, because in my mind it has been many katuns since I arrived here and since my suffering began?"

The angel said to him, "Understand that your torment had begun a short time ago; your body you left recently is not yet cold. For this reason, if you desire to enter into your body again and your torment for one year, after I say it for you, you will go quickly also."

Then the man said, "I desire more my torment for one year in my body, not to stay here for one day in this really severe torment because in my mind one hour lasts a year."

See the manner in which the torments of purgatory are very painful; the torments are truly unbearable of those who go there to do penance.[29]

29. In this last passage, "See the manner in which the torments of purgatory are very painful; the torments are truly unbearable of those who go there to do penance," we see one of the many occurrences of parallel construction. This stylistic device was

Nebuchadnezzar and the Fiery Furnace

The Maya story here is a retelling of three youths who refused to worship the idol of King Nebuchadnezzar—an account originating from the third chapter of Daniel in the Bible. As a result, the king threw them into a fiery furnace. Yet when he looked into the furnace, he saw not three but four persons. After realizing that God had sent a divine being to protect the youths, and after seeing that the youths were not harmed—"neither did it burn their beards nor their hair"—he understood the power of God in protecting his servants.

Although the story follows the biblical account rather closely, it betrays its Maya authorship in subtle ways. The text itself contains examples of parallel construction, which is a stylistic device employed by Maya (and Nahua) authors to rephrase what has been said in a different form. A simple example occurs as the text describes the king's reaction to the disobedience of the three youths: "The ruler was furious; he was really inflamed with rage." Other Maya-authored texts including the Chilam Balams and the Popol Vuh (a K'iche' Maya account of the world's creation) contain many examples of these constructions.[30]

EXCERPT FROM THE MORLEY MANUSCRIPT, 333–35

How We Should Have Strength and Obedience in the Law of God
It was written in the holy writings (scriptures) that an image was made by the ruler Nebuchadnezzar. When he finished making it, he ordered to be proclaimed and declared to the ears of the people the following: when the sounds of the flute and song are heard, everyone will come and bow their heads to worship the image the ruler made.

And all the people did it. Only three youths, who feared God, did not desire to worship the image. For this reason they were denounced before the ruler.

Then they were called by the ruler; he said to them, "Why will you not worship the image made by me? I am swearing to you, if you do not worship it, you will be cast into the oven and harshly

particularly common in early colonial native-language texts. This account is also found in Coronel, *Discursos predicables*, fols. 195r–96r.

30. For an intriguing study on parallelisms, see Sam Colop, "Poetics."

punished by me. Who is God to be able to free you from my hands?" said the ruler.

The youths said, "Understand that this God we have worshipped can remove us from your hands, and if he should not desire to save us from your hands, understand that never at any time will we worship your image."

Then the ruler was furious; he was really inflamed with rage because of the disrespectful words of the servants of God. He said to cast them into the oven, whose fire and burning is terrible. Nevertheless, his servants were not burned by the fire, nor did it do anything to them; instead, they were happy while they thanked God. The fire burned and killed only the many people that put the wood in and surrounded the oven.

When the ruler stood, the youths were seen; he saw four of them in there. He said, "Perhaps there were not only three that were cast into the oven; from where did the fourth appear?" Then the ruler said, "Ah, I have understood, here is the most esteemed true God, the God of these Christians. He alone is able to free his servants from affliction. Therefore, he freed his servants by sending his angel among them."

Then the youths were removed (from the oven) in perfect health, neither did it burn their beards nor their hair; truly the fire did nothing to them. This is the reason those people were amazed while they sighed, marveled because of it.

Now do you see how he is helped by our lord God, . . .[31] he that trusts in him?[32]

The Unrepentant Penitent

This story concerns a young woman whom everyone considered righteous for her pious works of good reputation. The young woman, however, kept secret from the community and her confessor an adulterous act she committed some time before. Upon her death, one of her friends asked God to show her whether the young women had gone to purgatory or heaven. The young woman then appeared to

---

31. The words are illegible and do not appear in Coronel's *Discursos predicables*.
32. See also Coronel, *Discursos predicables*, fols. 196r–97r.

her with a burning and grotesque face and declared her eternal damnation for not having confessed her sin.

The story is an altered rendition of one that appears, among
others, in a medieval book of exempla and again later in Sánchez's
The Book of Tales by A. B. C.[33] Here, the young woman is a French
nun, niece of the abbess, and very well respected. After frequently
associating with a good Christian man, they had sexual relations—
a sin she hid for fear of shame. After her death and a glorious burial,
the abbess and other nuns prayed to know the state of her spirit.
When the young nun appeared to them, she chanted and sang an
excerpt that appears to be from a responsory for the third nocturn
of Matins from the Office of the Dead, explaining how there is no
redemption in hell for those who sin and fail to repent. This the nuns
understood as her declaring her own damnation.

When comparing the stories, the first obvious difference concerns
the lack of nuns in the Maya rendition. But this is not overly surprising, considering that the first convent of nuns, Nuestra Señora de la
Consolación, was not established in Yucatan until 1596.[34] Given the
possibility that the Maya story was created sometime in the 1570s,
and likely in attempts to reach a wider audience, the author deemed
more appropriate the use of a young woman instead of a nun.
No doubt the author also saw this as an opportunity to address illicit
sexual relations among the general Maya population.

Another difference comes from the Maya story's emphasis on
the failure to confess the sin during confession itself. Although the
story states that confession has the power to wash away "one or two
years" of sin, even after the young woman went to confession "for
the second time . . . the third and fourth time; many times . . . with
her husband present and without her husband," she never divulged
the sin.[35] As a result of the omission, the young woman informs
the living of her condemned soul not through a specific responsory,

33. Today, the manuscript resides in Spain's Biblioteca Nacional and bears the title
"Exemplos y fábulas morales." For more on the manuscript and the story of the unre-
pentant woman, see Gayangos, *Escritores*, 443–48. See also Sánchez de Vercial, *Book of
Tales*, 59–60.

34. Rugeley, *Wonders and Wise Men*, 85–86; Restall, *Black Middle*, 55.

35. Morley Manuscript, 336, as appears in Whalen, "Annotated Translation."
There are a few interesting points here. First, the ability of the confession to absolve
one to two years of sin surely portrays the confessional experience for many faithful
Mayas who, due to overworked and overextended priests, would have the opportunity

which the Mayas would be unfamiliar with, but through a more visual image of her hideous and burning face. In general, the Maya author modifies the traditional story to suit an audience of neophytes in the Faith who required additional instruction on confession itself, its benefits and consequences, and the overall importance of being a "true Christian."

EXCERPT FROM THE MORLEY MANUSCRIPT, 335–38

Against Those Who Hide Their Sins from the Confessor
It really pains the devil when people confess all of their sins, because for this reason they are taken out from under the hands of the devils, and however many (sins) they achieve during one or two years of deceiving people, this goes away in an instant during that confession.

It was written in a book that there was a maiden whose works were very just and her reputation was very good within the town. When she went to confession[36] with the priest, she confessed her other sins, but she did not confess the concubinage that she had fallen into because her mouth was shut by the devil; she was ashamed to speak of, declare, and confess her mistake. When she went to confession for the second time, she buried it again. She did likewise on the third and fourth time. Many times she made a confession, with her husband present and without her husband, but she never told the priest of the mortal sin she earned as a child because of [her] holiness in the opinion of the people since she fasted, prayed, performed charity, and other good works.

When that woman died, there was one of her friends; this woman used to eat, walk, and talk with her, and she pleaded with God, saying, "Lord God, reveal to me where the friend was taken, perhaps to purgatory, or to heaven, because her Christianity was very loyal, in my opinion."

---

to confess only annually or semiannually. Second, confession was to be solely between the penitent and the confessor; the woman's husband should never have been present.

36. Although the word here, *confesar*, appears to be a rendition of the Spanish verb *confesar*, "to confess," the Maya author tends to favor the Maya *toh pul* for the verb "to confess." Thus, I translate it as a noun. Whalen does likewise for other reasons.

Not long after, the (dead) woman manifested herself with her face really burning and also very ugly, which frightfully surprised the woman, so that she said to the dead one, "It is not you, extinguish the fire!" Thus she said to her that was burning, and she said, "Perhaps I was not your friend? Therefore, why are you visiting this place as you are? Where were you taken to be given your torment?"

She said, "Ah, I am miserable because I was sentenced to reside forever in hell, and I am there below the feet of devils; I am only coming here to manifest myself to you because you asked it of God."

Then the woman said to her, "Why were you sentenced to go to hell? Where are the good works you performed previously? Where were they removed, your fasts, prayers, and works of charity?"

The dead one said, "Oh, I am desolate, a poor wretch because these, all my works you have mentioned here, were all in vain and they did nothing for me because I did not confess the mortal sin I committed previously as a child, and this is the reason I am sentenced to eternal ruin." Thus said the dead one; in that moment she disappeared.[37]

The Negligent Christian

This final tale instructs on the punishments that await the wicked. It speaks of a man who failed to adhere to Christianity and who was in his last extremity. As priests gathered around him to pray for his soul, he shouted for them to depart. He explained that a wild animal was torturing him and twisting his neck and that it would never finish killing him in the presence of the priests. Although the priests saw no such creature, they told him to cross himself. The man explained that his hands were pinned by the creature, so the priests wept and prayed over him. As a result, God freed the man from the wild animal's grasp, and the man reformed into a faithful Christian.

In the sixth-century *Dialogues* of Saint Gregory we find a tale with a similar story line and moral.[38] The story tells of a man who entered a monastery with no real intentions of taking the habit.

37. This story is also in Coronel, *Discursos predicables,* fols. 199v–200v. For a Nahuatl rendition of the tale, see Burkhart, "'Here Is Another Marvel.'"

38. Saint Gregory, *Dialogues,* 244–45.

As he lay dying of the plague, a dragon began to eat his head and coil around his body. After the monks prayed for him, the dragon fled and the man became a righteous monk. Again, the main differences between the Maya and European stories derive from a Maya author attempting to modify the story to reflect a Yucatecan colonial setting and make it more understandable to a native audience. In the process, the would-be monk becomes a man, the praying monks become priests, and the dragon becomes an *ah chibal*, "wild animal."

EXCERPT FROM THE MORLEY MANUSCRIPT, 346

As Man Lives, So He Dies
It was written in the writings of He of the nine souls,[39] Saint Gregory, that which occurred to a person who was frequently forgetful, negligent of his Christianity. When his death came, he began to shout out, while he said to the priests gathered before him, "Go away, you priests, leave alone the wild animal so that it finishes killing me because he is squeezing and twisting my neck with which he painfully tortures me; leave or he will never finish killing me. Go, for my sake, leave him alone to finish killing me," he said.

Then the priests were shocked because they never saw the wild animal he spoke of; they only heard the shout of the sick person. They said to the sick person, "Make the sign of the cross."[40]

Then he said, "I am not able to do it because my hand is bound by the wild animal."

At that time, the priests began to pray for the sick person with many tears. Then God desired to deliver him from the grasp of the wild animal, who was the devil. Because of this, he began to straighten his life and be diligent and careful in his Christianity.[41]

---

39. The phrase "He of the nine souls" derives from the Maya *ah bolon pixan*. The Mayas referred to some of their deities with the *ah bolon* prefix. Here, it is possible that the Mayas continued to use this prefix for what they might have perceived as the minor deities of Catholicism: the saints. See Christensen, *Nahua and Maya Catholicisms*, 46–48.

40. *Chicilbeza uich ti cruz* literally means "to sign or indicate the pattern of the cross."

41. The story is also in Coronel, *Discursos predicables*, fols. 201v–202r. Indeed, Whalen notes that only the final part of this story appears in the Morley Manuscript and that the initial section derives from Coronel's *Discursos predicables*.

3

Nahuatl and Maya Baptismal Texts

We establish and order that no curate nor religious nor priest administer the sacrament of baptism to any adult unless first he be sufficiently instructed in our holy Catholic faith.
—First Mexican Provincial Council, 1555

In Christianity, baptism is seen as the door that leads to discipleship and, eventually, salvation. The Bible records the words of Christ when teaching of the utmost importance of the sacrament in obtaining salvation. Speaking to the Pharisee Nicodemus, Christ instructed, "Verily, verily, I say unto thee, except a man be born of water and of the Spirit, he cannot enter into the kingdom of God."[1] The early friars of New Spain understood well the importance of baptism in their conversion efforts and, not surprisingly, it was the first sacrament administered to the Nahuas and Mayas.

The Franciscans were particularly enthusiastic advocates for the widespread administration of baptism. Many of the early Franciscans were strongly influenced by apocalyptic beliefs that viewed the Americas and its inhabitants as the final piece of a millenarian puzzle. According to their interpretation of biblical passages, the discovery of the Americas fulfilled apocalyptic prophecy. The natives, untouched by Protestantism and other "ailments" of Europe, would be the subjects of a perfected Christianity that would open the door for the Second Coming of Christ and the Final Judgment.[2] Thus, many Franciscans hastened to convert the natives and reported extraordinary numbers of converts. Fray Gerónimo de Mendieta stated that two Franciscans in Xochimilco reported having baptized fifteen thousand natives in one day.[3] Although surely exaggerated,

---

1. John 3:5 (AV).
2. For more on the Franciscans, their millenarian beliefs, and their evangelization of Mexico, see Phelan, *Millennial Kingdom*, and Baudot, *Utopia and History*.
3. Mendieta, *Historia eclesiástica indiana*, 159.

such numbers served a dual purpose. First, they connected the Franciscans to biblical apostles who, such as Peter, baptized thousands.[4] Second, they provided validation of the Franciscan's work in light of criticism from other orders, such as the Dominicans, who challenged the Franciscan's hold over New Spain's evangelization.

Certainly, these unbelievable numbers caused many ecclesiastics to wonder at the instruction each recipient received prior to baptism. The topic surfaced at the First Mexican Provincial Council in 1555 where religious authorities reasserted that all adults receive sufficient instruction prior to the rite.[5] To both adequately prepare Nahuas and Mayas for baptism and sufficiently educate them on the significance of the sacrament, ecclesiastics inserted into their religious works Nahuatl and Maya texts instructing the natives on baptism. In a book about religious texts, it seems only fitting that I include some of these texts. The following section contains translations from various published religious texts on the topic of baptism. Although each text similarly addressed the topic of baptism and its necessity for salvation, the instruction varied greatly from author to author and text to text.[6]

Huehuetlahtolli (Nahuatl)

Nahuatl had a form of rhetoric that was highly metaphorical, called *huehuetlatolli,* or "speech of the elders." Since the Nahuas traditionally used huehuetlatolli in moralistic discourses to encourage proper behavior, some of the early Franciscans and their native aides composed religious texts in this style in hopes that it would present Christian morals in a familiar way and encourage their acceptance.[7]

---

4. Acts 2:38–41.

5. Many works have discussed the controversy surrounding the Franciscan's methods of baptism. For example, see Pardo, *Origins of Mexican Catholicism,* 20–48; Christensen, *Nahua and Maya Catholicisms,* 126–32; and R. Ricard, *Spiritual Conquest,* 83–95.

6. Excerpts and further analysis of some of these texts can be found in Christensen, *Nahua and Maya Catholicisms,* 132–57.

7. For an overview of the collections of huehuetlatolli, see Sell, "Nahuatl Plays in Context," 14–15; for Sahagún's involvement with huehuetlatolli, see León-Portilla, *Bernardino de Sahagún,* 115–18. Another excellent example of early friars couching Christian teachings in native rhetorical devices is Sahagún's *Psalmodia christiana,* published in 1583. The work appropriated Nahua songs and inserted Christian messages, thus turning them into canticles sung to familiar precontact hymns. For a

In the 1530s fray Andrés de Olmos—a lead scholar at the College of Tlatelolco—collected and edited a variety of speeches in this metaphorical style that would later appear in fray Juan Bautista's published work *Huehuetlahtolli*. Included in Bautista's text were various huehuetlatolli discourses promoting Christianity and its practices, including baptism. Endorsers of the work credited Bautista with having "collected, amended, and augmented" its speeches, but in many cases it is difficult to determine what came from Olmos and what came from Bautista and his Nahua assistants.[8]

The following provides a wonderful example of how Nahuatl rhetoric and close ecclesiastic collaboration with Nahua assistants can shape a Christian discourse. In the text, parallel constructions and Nahua-specific expressions abound. Couching a Christian discussion on baptism into a rhetoric containing many indigenous metaphors and idioms can result in some unusual imagery. For example, the text states that Christ made the soul of the baptized "oquimochpuchtitzino: auh yequene ycihuanemactzin omuchiuh" (his bride, and additionally it [the soul] became his given woman). Admittedly, this passage could be translated a few ways. Typically, when *ichpochtli* is possessed it carries the meaning of "daughter," and Catholic belief holds that one becomes an adopted child of God during baptism. But most Nahuatl religious texts employ the possessed form of *pilli* when speaking of becoming a child of God through baptism, not the gendered *ichpochtli*.[9] Moreover, if we interpret the use of *ichpochtli* to mean "daughter," the passage would carry an incestuous meaning of Christ making the soul both his daughter and his given woman, or wife.

Another possibility, and the one I use, is that the author intended to use *ichpochtli* as "bride," or a young woman in the possession of another, in this case the bridegroom. This also seems to make sense

recent study on the precontact roots of the *Psalmodia christiana*, see Schwaller, "Pre-Hispanic Poetics," 315–32.

8. Bautista, *Huehuetlahtolli*, preliminary leaf, unnumbered. Regarding the nebulous matter of who contributed what, Baudot limits Bautista's influence to "small changes in details of style and a few scholarly corrections," while León-Portilla suggests Bautista's hand in composing the more Christian speeches included at the end of the work. See Baudot, *Utopia and History*, 230 but also 121–245, and León-Portilla, *Huehuetlahtolli*, 25–26.

9. In the subsequent texts of Sáenz de la Peña and Ignacio de Paredes, both authors speak of the ability of baptism to make the recipient a child of God, and both use variants of the phrase "tiypilhuā techmochihuilia in toTecuiyo Dios" (it [baptism] makes us children of our lord God).

when considering its pairing with *cihuanemactli*, or "given woman." In Nahua culture—and prior to the introduction of Christianity— nobles could take additional women other than their spouse. Although these women, the cihuanemactli, were not the principal wives of the noble men, Nahua society viewed the union as legitimate and acceptable.[10] Christianity, however, would view the union as adulterous. Perhaps the colonial author(s) chose *cihuanemactli* to represent a socially legitimate union instead of the Nahuatl word for spouse obtained through marriage, *namictli*, to prevent promoting the idea of dual spouses and thus polygamy; in other words the cihuanemactli of Christ could still be the namictli of someone else. Louise Burkhart noted a similar example in her work on Nahuatl Marian texts, *Before Guadalupe*. Here, Mary is the namictli of Joseph, but the *nemactli* of the Holy Spirit.[11] Interestingly, baptism was and is considered by Catholics to spiritually incorporate the recipient into the Body of Christ, or as a member of the church, which Saint Paul considered to be the bride of Christ. Indeed, in warning the congregations in Corinth about following false teachers, Saint Paul reminds his brethren, "I have espoused you to one husband, that I may present you as a chaste virgin to Christ."[12] Yet, in the end, the cihuanemactli still represents an adulterous union, and the rhetoric of the huehuetlatolli text allows for interpretations of questionable orthodoxy regarding the soul's relationship to Christ.

EXCERPT FROM FRAY JUAN BAUTISTA, *HUEHUETLAHTOLLI* (1600), FOLS. 71R–73R

Discourse Where It Is Explained the Great Good Man Achieves Through Holy Baptism.
Declaration That Explains the Very Great Fame, Honor That Is Acquired Through Holy Baptism.

O my younger sibling, O Christian, it is very necessary for you to frequently ponder on the very great, the very excellent fame, the

---

10. Motolinia, *Memoriales*, 323. See also Burkhart, *Slippery Earth*, 151. I thank Louise Burkhart for her insight in this matter. *Cihuanemactli* could also refer to a portion or inheritance that someone has as a woman, which can also amount to a woman's dowry. Yet I believe the intended religious meaning pushes the translation toward "given woman."

11. Burkhart, *Before Guadalupe*, 50–51.

12. 2 Cor. 11:2; for other examples, see 1 Cor. 6:15–17, 12:12–14; Matt. 22:1–14, 25:1–13; Eph. 5:25; Rom. 7:4; Gal. 3:27–28; Rev. 19:7–10 (AV).

honor bestowed on you when you were honored through baptism, and how when you had not yet received it, when baptism had not yet been performed on you, you were the slave, the subject of the devil,[13] Satan, and the devil was inside you, in your soul. Additionally, your soul was clouded, it was in the place of darkness,[14] and it was girt in sickness, it was carrying disease. But when you were baptized, then our savior Jesus Christ took up his home within you, in your soul, and at that time he illuminated it with his divine light, and he cured it with his grace, and he made it (the soul) his bride, and additionally it became his given woman. Thus, it is very necessary for you to do all you can to care for him, that you not expel him, that you not chase him from inside your soul, the ruler who surpasses all things.

Also, truly you must take great care that you do not lose or squander away the very great fortune, his grace, and that you perform and put in operation what is very necessary for you, that you should pursue, you should follow his path, I mean to say, how he lived on earth, never committing, performing sin. In the same way it is necessary for you to live on earth, not to go around frivolously committing sin, not to go about performing sin. Everything that has been mentioned is all written in the divine book (the Bible), for Saint Paul says it in the third chapter of his letter he wrote to the people of Galatia.

All of you who have been baptized in the churchly home (church) of our savior, Christ, you wrapped yourselves, you girded yourselves in the garments, the cloak of our savior Jesus Christ. That means that you vowed that for the whole time you live on this earth you will never sin, you will never commit sin, and you will keep the vow you made to take care of his grace he gave you, granted you through holy baptism. And this, God's grace, cannot be kept, cannot be cared for without first completely keeping, performing, exclusively focusing

---

13. For the devil, the author used the word *tzitzimitl*. *Tzitzime* were underworld deities associated with death, and their insertion within Nahuatl texts as a synonym for the devil was uncommon, particularly outside the sixteenth century.

14. The Nahuatl term here is *tlayohuayan*. Burkhart explains, "The term *tlayohuayan* 'in the place and/or time of darkness' was used in the Nahua-Christian literature in reference not only to dark underworlds but also to the time before the creation of the world, the time before the coming of Mary or Christ, the time before the coming of Christianity to the Nahuas, the state of idolatry or paganhood, and the state of sin. It is also applied to limbo in (Sahagún's) *Psalmodia*." *Holy Wednesday*, 223–24.

on the commandments of God, and without fleeing from, abandoning, fearing all mortal sins.

Regarding this, David also says in the twenty-ninth Psalm, "O our lord, my worry, my sadness you have turned into my joy, my consolation, and you have burst my carrying-sack[15] (relieved my burdens) and have encircled me with joy and pleasure."

It is necessary for the Christian to say these words every day in order to be thankful, grateful, for the benefits, the mercy that he was favored with on his baptism, because before he had been full of sadness, weeping, tears because of sin, and because of this God filled him up with his grace and joy, pleasure, and before he had been wrapped up in sin which had become like his clothes similar to that very stiff, very rough, and very worn-out carrying-sack he had worn. And he was given, girded with the garments of our savior, Jesus Christ, which is the Faith, truly it is necessary for him that was baptized to know and firmly believe in it, and it is especially necessary that he die in the Faith, and not in a way so that he abandons this Faith. It is necessary that each one separately believes, that each by himself believes, that is, not only is it necessary to believe all that our mother, the Holy Church, believes, but likewise to believe all that those credible sages in holy writing (scripture), who tell the truth, relate, and mention, and however many other things that are necessary to believe. Afterward, one's curiosity about this will be satisfied; afterward, you will see.

Fray Juan Bautista on John the Baptist (Nahuatl)

In 1606 fray Juan Bautista published a collection of sermons in his extensive *Sermonario*. In a sermon designed to be read on the third Sunday of Advent about the role of John the Baptist as the forerunner of Christ is a discourse that relates the difference between both John and Christ and the baptisms they offered.[16] According to

15. This is a particularly illustrative metaphor. Nahua commoners typically were burdened with carrying loads, particularly with the tumpline (a strap attached to a sack or backpack that was worn across the forehead). To say that baptism would relieve one's grief by bursting this sack of burdens would have resonated well with the Nahua audience. To indicate, as the text does, that David from the Old Testament made such a statement is a different matter entirely.

16. The season of Advent begins on the fourth Sunday before December 25.

the Bible, the difference is that baptism after the manner of Christ included a dedication to him and the gift of the Holy Spirit. Yet Bautista's text relates the difference between the two baptisms in a different way. The Nahuatl text chooses to emphasize the disparity in the social status of John and Christ. Specifically, the text employs terms and descriptions that represented two commonplace rankings in Nahua society: commoners and deities. John is described as an insignificant poor commoner, and Christ is referred to as Tloque Nahuaque, or "Lord of the Near and Close," which is an epithet for the precontact deity Tezcatlipoca. Although the self-perceived unworthiness of John is mentioned in the Bible, the Nahuatl text carries this much further. This modification, along with other rhetorical influences, again betrays the close collaboration with Nahua assistants the early Franciscans enjoyed. In the initial pages of his work, Bautista openly admits that various native assistants "have helped me in this work."[17] Such assistants no doubt are responsible for the rhetoric of the *Sermonario* that parallels precontact traditions of oral discourse while providing a Nahua version of a Christian theme.

EXCERPT FROM FRAY JUAN BAUTISTA,
SERMONARIO (1606), FOLS. 583V–584R

"I baptize with water. But in your midst has stood one whom you do not know. He is the one who will come after me, who was made before me, the strap of whose sandal I am not worthy to untie."[18]
It means, "I merely baptize with water. One will follow me, who before I was a man, before I possessed reason, was a man first, exercised reason first, he is so great that I do not deserve to remove his sandals, to loosen the straps of his sandals."
It is as though Saint John means, "I merely bathe, clean people with water, but understand that the Savior is already among you, and you do not see him, you do not recognize him; I am only his messenger, the one who goes before him, his announced; he is

17. Bautista then goes on to list eight in particular: Hernando de Ribas, don Juan Bernardo, Diego Adriano, don Francisco Bautista de Contreras, Esteban Bravo, don Antonio Valeriano, Pedro de Gante, and Augustín de la Fuente. Prologue to *Sermonario*, preliminary leaf, unnumbered. For a description of these assistants, see Burkhart, *Holy Wednesday*, 68–70.
18. Original in Latin. This quote is derived from Matthew 3.

already coming, he will appear, you will see and recognize him;
he became a man and attained reason before I was a man and possessed reason, for he greatly surpasses me, for he is God, for he is
the Lord of the Near and Close. I am merely a poor commoner, I am
an insignificant person, I am nothing, and not worthy even though
I should loosen his sandal strings, even to go about carrying his
sandals, or even to serve him by some truly despicable task. When
he comes, he will dispense baptism by which people will be saved;
my baptism merely counts as a preparation. May you not be angry
with me, merely gladly, patiently await his mercy."

This, then, is how it is seen that God's beloved, Saint John, very
truly performed and completed his duty for which our lord God
appointed him so that he became his announcer, so that he made
the people on the earth acquainted with him (Christ), so that he
proclaimed to them, to be prepared, to receive him, and because of
his mercy, his salvation, they will be happy. And although the Jews
greatly opposed him (Saint John), he was not at all perturbed but all
the more he acknowledged and exalted him (Christ) right in the presence of many Jews.

Texts from a Secular Priest and a Jesuit (Nahuatl)

Although some baptismal texts were brief and to the point, others
were much more comprehensive and informative. Baptismal texts
maintained their popularity as the colonial period progressed and
ecclesiastics remained concerned regarding the natives' comprehension of the sacrament and the tenets of Christianity in general. This
is seen in the mid- and late colonial texts of the secular priest Andrés
Sáenz de la Peña and the Jesuit Ignacio de Paredes. The elegant and
descriptive metaphoric prose seen in the earlier Franciscan works
appears only sporadically in these two texts. As mentioned, this is
likely the result of a steady decrease in native collaboration or the
genre in general, or both. Indeed, it is surprising that Paredes's 1759
text contains such rhetorical elements at all. He himself explains this
anomaly, stating that instead of using contemporary eighteenth-
century Nahuatl, which he termed to be "barbarous," he used (or
at least attempted to use) the "genuine" version of the language

that classical authors, such as fray Alonso de Molina and Bautista, employed.[19]

Both baptismal texts choose to emphasize the sacrament's meaning, effect, and administration. Emphasis seems to be placed on helping Nahuas understand the significance of the sacrament and one's responsibility afterward. Paredes's text in particular provides informative details that describe the origination of the sacraments in general, baptism and all its effects, the role of godparents, and even an anecdote about a dying Nahua whose miraculous vision of heaven led to his baptism by two Jesuit priests immediately prior to his death. Interestingly, and similar to the huehuetlatolli text, Paredes instructs the baptized that they become the property of Christ, but, as the reader will see, he goes about it in a much more orthodox and conventional way that omits any mention of cihuanemactli.

EXCERPT FROM ANDRÉS SÁENZ DE LA PEÑA, *MANUAL DE LOS SANTOS SACRAMENTOS* (1642), FOLS. 33R–36R

Consider and ponder on it with very great prudence. My beloved children, that which we do here is to perform spiritually the perfectly marvelous sacrament called baptism; it precedes and is taken first because really no one earthly human whosoever can be saved without first being baptized.

For so it is in the order that our beloved Redeemer spoke to his beloved disciples, "Go, all over the world and teach the people of the earth, open their eyes, baptize them in the name of God the Father, the Son, and the Holy Spirit; and all creation, whoever will believe and is baptized will be saved, but whoever will not believe will be entirely damned, condemned."

Through the sacrament of baptism and the divine amelioration of the divine Holy Spirit, we are spiritually reborn so that we live anew for the first time. With it the other sacraments begin and are founded, and it removes all the bad that is in one's spirit, soul, and entirely gathers all that is good, delights, and enriches. Wherefore all sin, or original sin, or mortal sin, even though really frightening and unmentionable, disappears because of the purification and

19. Paredes, *Promptuario manual mexicano*, preliminary leaf, unnumbered.

the strengthening of the sacrament of baptism. This water of life not only cleans one, removes the dirt and blackness of sin,[20] but likewise because of it we are forgiven all the suffering that would have been the punishment of sin. And one's spirit and soul is filled with goodness, grace that turns us completely good and it makes us children of our lord God so that we will attain happiness in heaven. And the purifying virtues emerge from and take root in it (baptism) so that one's spirit and soul is enriched, delighted. And baptism spiritually pertains to our lord Jesus Christ's beloved, honored head so that the body of our honored mother Holy Church is made; and our lord Jesus Christ is the true eternal fountain of life from which really gushes all divine amelioration, *grace*, and likewise from there emerges the power with which all that pertains to Christianity can be done.

And in the same way it places on our spirits, souls, a mark of richness as in those who have been gifted by our lord Jesus Christ. This mark never ever disappears; if the sacrament of baptism has already been received once, it cannot be received again. Afterward, the sacrament of baptism opens up for us the entryway to heaven—which had been fully closed because of sin—so that we can enter the place of supreme happiness, blessedness, glory, where we will be entirely happy and live forever where there is never affliction, suffering.

Very many things are done during the baptism that inaugurated the disciples and the prophets of our lord Jesus Christ; wherefore we are to honor his marvelous works not only with words, but likewise with deeds which inspire us and move our spirits to imprint it very strongly on our memories. Those that are to be baptized are detained at the entryway to the church because if they are not first freed from the labor and service of the devil, and if they do not first bow down to the rulership of our lord Jesus Christ, they cannot attain entry into the home of God (the church).[21] And there they are given

20. Here and throughout many other religious texts, sin is equated with filth and blackness. European ecclesiastics made frequent use of this rhetoric to describe sin as a sickness and pollution of the soul. In the Americas, this rhetoric continued within native-language religious texts and often found support from preexisting concepts of filth and impurity and their effects. But native cultures, such as the Nahua, understood the existence and consequence of such impurities within a native frame of mind that varied from that of the ecclesiastics. For more on the subject, see Burkhart, *Slippery Earth*, 87–129.

21. This passage refers to the exorcisms (scrutinies) natives were to receive prior to baptism. These prayers of exorcism continue today in the baptismal rite.

names so that always they will remember that they have been made persons of honor, warriors, and that they belong to the banner of our lord Jesus Christ and they take part in his war. Likewise through the book teaching proper living (the scriptures) they are taught how our lord Jesus Christ instructed us upon his departure so that those of advanced age (adults) will understand what to acknowledge and likewise what their duty and obligation will be; for small children that cannot speak, their godparents are responsible.

The words of blessing are followed through with good words, and they are performed with prayer so that the devil will be chased away and evicted from where he resided inside the soul of the one baptized. Salt is placed in his mouth so that he can be freed from nauseous sin; likewise, so that he is able to savor the divine wisdom of our lord God. Saliva is placed on his ear and nose so that people will take an example from the miracle our lord Jesus Christ performed when he cured the blind man with spit-clay he (Christ) placed on his eyes, and our lord Jesus Christ ordered him to immediately wash his eyes with water from Siloam,[22] which well signified the sacrament of baptism. With the holy oil and holy chrism it anoints him like a warrior so that he will remember that he is a Christian and follow in the footsteps of our lord Jesus Christ through his just life and good deeds, for the name "Christian" came right from Christ. And a white cloth and also the light, the burning candle, that is placed in the hands of the baptismal candidate signifies the pure life he will go along maintaining forever, and the light which he will always go about radiating; and he will live here on earth with good deeds and signs of a just life.[23]

This is what the sacrament of baptism does and effects, and through the many things we truly declared regarding it, all should really understand how with much reverence, much humility this sacrament is to be received; likewise concerning it (baptism), we should

22. See John 9:6–7.

23. Pope Paul III issued a papal bull in 1537, attempting to clarify the necessary pomp and ceremony that should accompany baptism. Traditionally, this would include the use of holy water, salt, saliva, candles, the white garment, and the oil of both the chrism and catechumens. Because the early Franciscans complained that it would be impossible to use all such items on every native, Paul III allowed ecclesiastics to use the salt, saliva, cloth, and candles for two or three natives who would represent all others in attendance, although he expected each native to be anointed with oil and chrism. But variation continued to exist among ecclesiastics. Here, Sáenz de la Peña explains the significance of such items.

remember how much the obligation will be of those who there vowed to recognize the love and great mercy of the sole deity, the ruler God, so that we belong to his Faith; and likewise how at the baptismal spring (baptistery) we are entirely purified; not because we deserve or merit it, but just because of the all-encompassing, never-ending, perfect great goodness of our lord God. May he be forever praised, glorified, exalted, and honored. May it be done (amen).

EXCERPT FROM IGNACIO DE PAREDES, *PROMPTUARIO* (1759), 242–50

When the all powerful God originally created this entire earth, my children, also, at that very moment in the beginning of the world, he made a really pleasing flower garden, a really pleasant enclosed garden, Paradise,[24] where we would be living happily if the first humans had not sinned (*the first humans, origin of the human race*) our first parents, Adam and Eve: *However, the lord God had planted a garden of pleasure from the beginning in which he placed the man whom he had formed (Genesis 2:8)*.[25] And where from underground in the place of flowers a very great river came gushing and springing forth that later divided into four parts (*a river, which was divided in four*). And that river watered and irrigated the whole world. *And the river was going out from the place of pleasure to water the garden, which was then divided into four sources (V. 10)*.[26] Superlative, my children, was the divine place of flowers, the enclosed garden our lord Jesus Christ made. That was the Holy Church; for he established and left for us seven divine fountains, seven divine rivers that always are gushing, drizzling, springing forth (*they are always flowing seven fountains*) with which we wash ourselves and recover from our sins, and because of which we become good and pure before God. And that divine fountain of eternal life,

24. Paredes's description of the paradise of the Garden of Eden as a place of flowers would resonate with Nahua ideas of a paradisiacal afterlife in either Tlalocan or Tonatiuhilhuicac, as flowers abounded in both places. See León-Portilla, *Aztec Thought and Culture*, 124–26.

25. Original in Latin. Stafford Poole provided the Latin translations and notes that the passages are on the whole quite accurate and agree with the Latin Vulgate, indicating that Paredes or native assistants penned the citations from the Vulgate and not from memory, as is sometimes done.

26. Original in Latin.

my children (*fountain of eternal life*), is the seven divine remedies, betterments, sacraments[27] that our savior Jesus Christ left us upon dying; and now we will speak concerning them.

First of all you should understand, my children, that our lord Jesus Christ, when he was living here on this earth, himself and in person put in order, established (*established*) these seven remedies, betterments, sacraments; where he was able to seal up and assign to them (the sacraments) all his treasure from his torment, his death, and innumerable merits with which we can help ourselves, be forgiven as sinners, and truly be saved however very horrid our sins may be because really very great is the power, strength, and efficacy of the sacrament (*it is very great the power and efficacy of the sacrament*); it immediately destroys and returns as nothing all sin, evil, and wickedness.

And this is because of these divine marvels, sacraments, called divine remedies, divine betterments (*remedies that cure us and justify, or make us good*). It means, my children, that we should see and consider the sacraments that remedy and improve, as if they were a divine medicine with which we heal and save ourselves from any divine sickness of our spirits and souls, which is sin. And when no sin is any longer attached to our souls, in that case the purifying sacrament strengthens our spirits, increases and multiplies in us divine goodness and purity, *grace*, with which we become especially pure and beautiful before God (*with grace we are rendered more clean and beautiful before God*).

And so that we understand, my children, what the sacrament does for our souls, our lord Jesus Christ comes to show us, he places before us an evident example; he indicates to us and makes us acquainted with what the sacrament achieves and does for our souls; as we see when someone is baptized, my children, that the priest pours water on his head. That means and signifies that as water washes us, we are bathed by it and cleansed from our filth, dirt, and grime (*of our dirtiness*), in the same way divine baptism washes us and purifies our spirits of the dirt, the grime, the putrefaction of our souls.

27. Here, Paredes employs a bilingual triplet construction to describe a "sacrament" as "teoyotica tepatiloni, teyectililoni, sacramentos" (divine remedies, betterments, sacraments).

And we should understand, my children, that baptism by no means performs that great miracle for us because of just the water itself, but it is because of and through (*by means of*) the sign appearing in it that our lord Jesus Christ assigns us and makes our own (*assigns to us and makes our property*) his precious revered boon with which we are cured, become good, and are saved. However, it is true, my children, that in order to obtain this our help, this our forgiveness of sins, and this our salvation given to us we really need to receive the sacraments that bring remedy through good preparation. Because if we do not do this, my children, the sacrament will not avail us, it will not help us, but thereby we will greatly sin and offend our lord our ruler, God.

Now may we presently understand, my children, "what thing is divine baptism?" Regarding this, the teaching aid, catechism, answers us thus, "It is a divine birth, it gives us divine purification, grace, and it is the sign of the Christian." That means, my children, that when we are baptized, we are spiritually born again. Because even though we were already born once in body through our mothers, truly, my children, we were born in sin. Although our earthly bodies were living, our souls were not living at all in the divine sense, but were dying in the divine sense because of original sin, which reached us right away inside the wombs of our mothers when we were engendered and conceived (*we contracted original sin from the first instant of our conception*). And because of this we were born enemies to God, and we are the children, prisoners, and slaves of the devil in hell. And so, if we had died that way, we would not have been saved at all and would never at all enjoy God in heaven.

Truly, my children, when we are baptized right away our souls come to life and are spiritually reborn. Right away God forgives us every one of our sins, and by his hands we are freed from the devil in hell. Right away God gives us divine purification, divine approval, grace, and everything to make good and purify with which we can spiritually live for the first time. Right away God also adopts us as his children and makes eternal rejoicing in heaven, glory, ours. And also at that very time God places on our souls a spiritual mark (*a mark*) with which we are marked and set apart from unbelievers, non-Christians, and then we belong to the Faith of our lord Jesus Christ; we also then become the children of the Holy Church, and then we are helped by the various good works Christians perform, and also then we are able to receive every remedy, the sacraments, that those unbaptized cannot receive.

Therefore, we should understand, my children, that baptism is as if it were the door to the Holy Church, because of which we are counted as among its believers, and it is like the door to heaven, because no one can be saved if he is not baptized. *Unless someone will have been born again of water and the Holy Spirit, he cannot enter into the kingdom of God (John 3:5).*[28] And because of this, my children, really take care so that all your children will be baptized, and let no one die unbaptized, and so that you perform this baptism as I told and announced to you in the teaching aid, the catechism, that everyone, whether male or female, adult or child, who is of the age of reason,[29] can baptize someone when they are in great need since the child is about to die and is not able to be taken to the church and no priest has been found to baptize him. Inspect and look into the matter there (in the catechism) (*review it there*) so that you can correctly perform the baptism.

Regarding this, you should understand, my children, that immediately it erases forever not just all the original sin, and every other sin whatever it may be that attaches to him who is baptized; also immediately it erases and lessens the punishment of sin that he would endure either here on earth or in the place of purification, purgatory, because of his sins. And so, if an adult, a person with reason, although he had been a most frightful sinner, if through faith and repentance he is baptized and dies right away, it is really very true and correct that he will immediately go straight to heaven, because through his baptism God has forgiven him not only all his sins, but also he has relieved him of his punishment he would have to pay (*that he had to pay*) and endure because of his sins. And any person, although a great sinner, that was baptized, at that time it is no longer necessary for him to confess nor do anything else to be forgiven, but only that he serve God and carry out what before God he promised and swore. Which is that he completely rejected all sin, the devil, and all devilish things (*all devilish things*), and also he swore that he would serve, love, and obey the really only one true deity, God.

28. Original in Latin.
29. This would be any adolescent or adult.

May we always remember our promise we made in our baptism, my children, and may we maintain it within our hearts so that we will never spoil or transgress against it. May we consider, my children, that God marked us in our baptism; he wrote on our souls, placed on them his mark, because of which really we belong to him and really we are his property (*we pertain to and are only of God*). And this mark of God (*character*) on us, we should understand, my children, that it never will leave or disappear but will be forever placed on our souls. And because of this, never ever can we be baptized twice, never twice can we receive this sacrament of baptism. But really only once can we be baptized, really only once can we be spiritually born, as really only once we were born in the flesh on this earth (*we are to be born spiritually one time, as one time we were born according to the flesh to the world*). Thus, my children, one who is baptized twice or three times will commit a really monstrous sin.

It only remains (*we only lack*), my children, for us to speak about spiritual fathers and mothers, who are the godfathers and godmothers who carry the child in their arms to the church in order to speak for it and answer the priest for the child when he questions the child concerning the baptism he is about to administer. And concerning this we should know, my children, that is the great obligation of spiritual fathers, godfathers and godmothers, that they know the holy words, spiritually raise (*indoctrinate*) and cause to live well their spiritual children, those whom they have baptized, those whom they have adopted (*to those whom they baptized or had in baptism*).[30] How can it be otherwise, for they assumed the spiritual duty when at the baptism of the child they took it and carried it in their arms and before the Holy Church adopted it (*adopted it*). However, it is true that if the actual parents of the child do and carry out that spiritual duty, then it is no longer the obligation of the spiritual fathers to do and perform this.

Likewise, we really need to know, my children, that the one who became the spiritual father or mother of a child truly became spiritually related to that child and his father and mother (*the godfather became related to the godchild, and his father and mother*); he[31]

---

30. Eighteenth-century texts frequently spoke about the responsibilities of godparents. As ecclesiastics continued to realize the shortcomings in their evangelization efforts, it appears that they increasingly relied on the assistance of godparents. The Council of Trent similarly had placed an emphasis on the role of godparents.

31. Could also be "she" in reference to the godmother.

(the godparent) became their relative; thus he cannot by any means marry the person he baptized, his spiritual child, neither (*neither*) can he (the godparent) marry the child's parents, for they are his *compadre* and *comadre*.[32] But he can marry the others although they are the children of his *compadres*, perhaps the older brothers or younger siblings of his spiritual child, the one he baptized (*but the godparents surely can marry the siblings of their godchild*).[33]

Here, my children, is everything that pertains to this very marvelous remedy, the sacrament of baptism. Now hear its power, by which we can be saved and enter into heaven (*P. Pérez History of the Provenance of Mexico*):[34]

In some altepetl here in the kingdom of Mexico two religious of the Company of Jesus arrived and asked the commoners (indigenous people) who were inhabitants of the altepetl if there was any sick person that they could help.

The altepetl residents answered them, "There is no one any longer (*there is not a single sick person any longer*), because there was one sick person and he died yesterday."

The religious were concerned, and went to enter the sick person's home, and they saw that he had not yet died but was in the last extremity. The religious encouraged the sick person a bit and then taught him all that he really needed to be saved. Afterward they asked the sick person if he desired to be baptized and if he rejected all his sins.

Immediately the sick person answered them, "Yes, I desire to be baptized and I reject all sin, even though I believe I have never sinned."

After the poor, sick indigenous person was baptized he told a religious, "You should know, my father, that when I began to be sick two perfectly beautiful and radiant people entered where I was. I do not know where they took me, but I beheld a palace, a place to give people great happiness, where many people were seated. And when I tried to sit down in a particular one of the seats that was empty

---

32. During baptism, the biological parents and godparents of a child became ritual co-parents, or *compadres*.

33. The possibility of sexual relations between godparents, godchildren, and their biological parents long concerned central Mexican and Yucatecan ecclesiastics, whose native-language confessional manuals nearly always included questions concerning the matter.

34. The subsequent tale, as indicated by the text, derives from Andrés Pérez de Ribas's 1645 *Historia de los triumphos de nuestra santa fee*. See *History*, 671–72.

(*in an empty seat*), the people restrained me and told me, 'You cannot yet sit down here until you are baptized. Therefore hurry, go to your home, for two religious will arrive there who will baptize you so that you can immediately return here to heaven.' "

When the poor commoner had said this, he died immediately. Here, my children, is how we really need baptism in order to attain divine purification, grace, and rejoicing in heaven, glory. O Jesus, may it be done (amen).

Fray Juan Coronel on Baptism (Maya)

Very few Maya texts known today contain the general topic of baptism, and those that do are rather brief. Despite their brevity, the Maya texts included here are some of the most extensive on the topic of baptism. They derive from the Franciscan Juan Coronel's 1620 *Discursos predicables* and are included as part of a larger discussion on the sacraments of the church and a speech given to the baptized. Much of the detail found in Nahuatl texts escapes Coronel's discussion, which instead focuses largely on relating the responsibilities of parents and their compadres, who serve as godparents to their child.[35] The necessary assistance of godparents in ensuring the Christian upbringing of Maya children surely would have been important to those few friars tasked with evangelizing the Yucatan. When compared with the Nahuatl texts, this simple and brief Maya text reminds us yet again of the rich diversity of baptismal texts written for Nahuas and Mayas.

EXCERPT FROM FRAY JUAN CORONEL, *DISCURSOS PREDICABLES* (1620), FOLS. 215V–216R, 220V–221R

Baptism
The first sacrament is baptism,[36] by which the child's soul is washed and his/her sin is forgiven by God.

---

35. Although baptism likewise renders the biological parents compadres to the godparents, the text uses *compadre* to refer specifically to the godfather.

36. Coronel uses a variety of terms to translate "baptism." Here he uses *caput çihil*, "twice born." Other times he uses *haa tu pol*, "water on the head."

Do you know who is wicked? Now, baptism is necessary for all of us because of the sin of our first parents; this is the reason. The child who dies without baptism will never see nor please God. So said our Redeemer to Nicodemus a truth he says to you, "Whoever is not baptized with water and the Holy Spirit cannot enter the kingdom of God," he said.

At the baptism first a man is appointed to hold the child at the basin and alone answer the priest's words. However, the compadre answers on his (the child's) behalf, in which he will say he/she desires baptism and to enter into Christianity [and] "I desire to eternally hate the devil and his dangerous path." Then he answers the remaining words asked by the priest.

This is why the child is cradled by the compadre, who really knows the cradled child, and its father and its mother too. Not just anyone for the child. What, a common person is granted the privilege of *compadrazgo*?[37] No, a person with much discernment and who is a true Christian will be granted the privilege.

Speech for the Baptized [220v]
You children. You children who are baptized. You become the children of God because of the holy sacrament, baptism. Therefore, hurl yourselves to God by being good Christians with deeds and works in the service of the Ruler.[38]

When you grow you will be diligent teachers of the doctrine and that which God calls good; the teacher tells his children what God really expects of man, and his deeds and works are in the service of the Ruler.

But as for you, compadre, see that you reconcile yourself as the godfather of your godchild so that you really get to know and bond with each other, and the father and mother also. You will never be able to marry your godchild or its mother because you are a spiritual parent. But therefore you will offer friendship to one another.

---

37. Compadrazgo is the ties of ritual kinship between godparents and biological parents, or ritual co-parenthood. For more on the Mayas' involvement with and application of the compadrazgo system, see Thompson, *Tekanto*, 216–20; and Farriss, *Maya Society*, 257–59.

38. The Ruler originates from *ah tepal*, "one who reigns, governs, is powerful, provides shelter." Occurring throughout colonial Maya texts, the term is frequently employed when referring to God but can also be used for secular rulers.

However, the compadre is the only one who holds the child at the basin while the water is poured on his head; he who cradles the children is not joined by any other.[39]

Understand me or you will be negligent. Godfathers, godmothers,[40] teach your cradled child the doctrine; you future teachers will become culpable.

Instructions for Emergency Baptisms (Nahuatl)

Baptism is such an important ordinance in Catholicism that provisions were made to accommodate those circumstances in which a person on the verge of death could be baptized by someone other than a priest. Throughout the colonial period, epidemics and high rates of infant mortality made this exception rather commonplace. Because priests were few and far between, ecclesiastics trained Nahua and Maya assistants to administer baptism in their absence and in cases of emergency. To ensure the natives performed the emergency baptism correctly, select authors inserted instructions into their religious texts. Two Nahuatl texts included here provide excellent examples of these instructions. The first is from fray Alonso de Molina's 1569 *Confessionario mayor*; the second is from Paredes's 1758 translation of Gerónimo de Ripalda's *Doctrina christiana*, which also contained his own instructions on emergency baptism.[41] The two texts share many similarities, but also some differences in their prescribed execution of the baptism. Moreover, the rhetoric of Molina's text betrays a mastery of Nahuatl prose no doubt obtained with the assistance of his native aide(s). Nearly two hundred years later Paredes attempted to mimic such mastery in his text, but he is only somewhat successful.[42] With regard to the Mayas, although native assistants were trained in and performed emergency baptisms,

---

39. Existing documentation for the colonial Mayas suggests that they favored the compadre tie between men. See Restall, *Maya World*, 102; and Farriss, *Maya Society*, 258.

40. These terms can also refer to "fathers" and "mothers," but because they fall within a treatise designated, as Coronel states, for godparents, I have translated them as such.

41. Ripalda, *Catecismo mexicano*, preliminary leaf, unnumbered.

42. For a discussion on Paredes's attempts at a purist text and his shortcomings, see Sell, "Friars, Nahuas, and Books," 235–45.

no Maya texts exist (of which I am aware) detailing the sacrament's
emergency performance.

EXCERPT FROM FRAY ALONSO DE MOLINA,
CONFESSIONARIO MAYOR (1569), FOLS. 21V–25R

Have you baptized some child who was about to die? Or perhaps you
did not declare well the divine words with which people are baptized?
Do you know them? Did you do all things that the Holy Church
commands you concerning baptism? Did you do all things I am about
to tell you here?

Here is given in what manner they will baptize, those who are
in charge of baptism will baptize when someone is about to die.
It is necessary that those who baptize children who are about to
die, in order to do their duty and not go against the charge that our
mother, the Holy Church, gives them, should remember and do five
things.

First, whoever you are that is about to baptize someone, whether
you are a man or a woman, you must understand that your only
obligation is to baptize a child or someone in the age of reason who is
about to die. You cannot baptize one who is strong and can be taken
before a priest. If you baptize a strong person, thereby you will sin
greatly, you will incur in mortal sin, because it is the charge and duty
of priests alone to baptize people and administer the sacrament called
baptism and the other sacraments. And those who are not priests are
charged only with baptizing children or those in the age of reason
who are about to die, who can no longer be taken before priests
because the church is distant, and if they try to take them there, they
will die on the way.

Second, your obligation is that you will baptize with plain water
not blessed, nor is it necessary for you to bless it. And although
there is blessed water that a priest has blessed, called sanctified water
[blessed] with chrism, it is not your charge to baptize someone
with it because you will sin greatly if you baptize someone with it,
because it is for priests alone to baptize someone with blessed water.
And if the child is about to die immediately and no plain water is
there, if there is consecrated water that we call blessed water, that the
priest blesses once a week, you can baptize with it. And if there is no
blessed water, if there is sanctified water, then that is your obligation

to take it quickly and baptize the one who is about to die. You are
to say, "*ego te baptizo*," etc., as is explained in the fifth part of your
obligation, which will be given later. And if nonblessed water can be
found quickly, only with it will you baptize someone, because it is
not your obligation to take or touch the sanctified water blessed with
chrism. If there is other water not blessed with chrism, even though
it should be merely lime water, even though it should not be very
clean, the child can be baptized with it.

Third, your obligation is to baptize a child who is still alive,
whose soul has not yet departed, even though he is breathing his last
breath. You are not to baptize someone who has really died, whose
soul has really departed, who no longer moves, for in that you will
sin. And if you do not know whether the child is alive or has really
died, it is necessary that you baptize him. And in order to baptize
him, you are to say, "If you have died, I do not baptize you, but if
you are alive, *ego te baptizo*," etc. And if he is not fully born, if a
living child's hand or foot has come out and appeared, then you are
quickly to pour water on his hand or his foot and you will say, "*Ego
te baptízo in nómine patris, et fílii, et spíritus sancti. Amen.*" And if
only his head has appeared, you are to baptize that; you are to cover
with a cloak the body of a woman who is bearing a child and giving
birth. And if afterward the child is fully born, whose foot or hand
you baptized for him, they are quickly to take him before a priest so
that he can baptize him as our mother, the Holy Church, commands.
And if you baptized his head, it is no longer necessary for him to
be baptized again when he has been fully born. And this matter the
priest will consider, whether the one who baptized the child pronounced the baptismal words properly, etc. Because if he pronounced
them well, as is required, the priest will not baptize him again at all.
But if he did not pronounce them [correctly], it is necessary for the
priest to baptize him right away.

Fourth, when you are about to baptize him it is your charge that
first you will say to yourself, "What I am about to do now, our
mother, the Holy Church, wants and commands me." And when you
have said this, immediately you are to baptize the child who is not
yet able to be born or has been born already.

Fifth, it is necessary for you to know very well the holy words
with which people are baptized so that you will not spoil the baptism.
Because if you do the baptismal words wrong, you will sin greatly

thereby and you will not provide a true baptism; the child will not be saved thereby, and you will baptize him in vain. Because of this you have a very great obligation to learn well and state very well the baptismal words with which the Holy Church baptizes people. You are to baptize in Latin or Nahuatl. You are to say, "*Ego te baptízo in nómine patris, et fílii, et spíritus sancti. Amen.*" And if you baptize in Nahuatl, you are to say, "*Nimitzquatequia yca yn itocatzin tetatzin, yhuan tepiltzin, yhuan spiritu sancto. Amen.*"[43] And then you are to begin to pour water on the head of the child, and you are to stop when you finished the holy words; no longer are you to pour the water. You are only to make the holy words accompany your pouring water on the head of the child or his hand or foot.

And before you begin to baptize the child, first, you will name him Pedro or María, etc. You are to say, "*Pedro or Maria, ego te baptízo in nómine patris, et fílii, et spíritus sancti. Amen.*" And if you want to baptize in Nahuatl, you are to say, "*In tiJuan {anoço} yn tiFrācisca nimitzquatequia, yca yn itocatzin tetatzin yuan tepiltzī yuan spiritu sancto Amen.*"[44] And if you are about to baptize and cannot tell whether it is a male or female, you are not to call it anything, but say to yourself, "Now I want to baptize whatever child is about to be born as our mother, the Holy Church, commands me." And if the one you baptized does not die right away, it is necessary they take it to the church so that the priest will put oil and chrism on it, etc.

And you who baptizes, if you do all these things mentioned here, thereby you will become very deserving before our lord; you will see a very great reward in heaven because you helped your fellow man so that he was saved and because of you he obtained, he saw our lord God's grace. And if you should not baptize as you were told here, and if you should forsake your obligation because of laziness, you will place yourself in great danger, and because of this the Giver of Life will punish you because you did not help, you did not show mercy on him whom you could have mercy on, you could have helped if you had wanted to.

---

43. "I baptize you in the name of the Father and the Son and the Holy Spirit. Amen."

44. "Juan or Francisca, I baptize you in the name of the Father and the Son and the Holy Spirit. Amen."

EXCERPT FROM *CATECISMO MEXICANO*, TRANSLATED AND
EDITED BY IGNACIO DE PAREDES (1758), 164–69

Here Is Given How People Will Be Baptized
When They Are in Great Need
We very greatly need and would be greatly satisfied by [it]. When
some child who has not yet been saved is in extremity and will die
very soon, and no priest appears to baptize it, in truth at that time
any person at all, whoever it might be—whether Spaniard or indigenous person, male or female, adult or child, if it has reached the age
of reason—anyone can baptize that child so that it will be saved. And
likewise if no other person is there to baptize it, it could even be the
father or mother of the child, they can baptize it, for so God advises
us. If we do not do this when someone really needs it, we will greatly
offend God.

It is like this: if the child is in the last extremity, let whoever it
should be, as long as they have the use of reason, baptize it right
away. But first, you Christian, open your eyes or prick up your
ears so that you will see or hear how you are to correctly perform
the baptism. First of all, you will get in the right frame of mind to
do that which our mother Holy Church wants concerning baptism,
which is for the child to become a Christian and belong to the Faith
of our lord Jesus Christ so that he will be saved. Here is what you are
to say even if just to yourself before you baptize someone: "My God,
I determine to perform that which the Holy Church wants concerning baptism. I desire that this your creature become a Christian so
that he will be saved and eternally make you happy." Then you will
go to get some water of any kind, even if it is not holy water, and
gladly, calmly pour it on the head of the child. And when you begin
to baptize him, also at that same time you will pronounce the holy
baptismal words, because the holy words will greatly join, unite, and
guide, and each little thing will not come out separately.

Here are the holy words you are to pronounce when you begin
to baptize someone. If a male, you are to name him Joseph or Juan
or another male name; if a female, you are to name her María or
Anna or another female name. But if you do not know whether it is
a little boy or girl, then you are to not to name it anything because
the name is not entirely necessary for the baptism to turn out good.
Afterward, pour the water on the child which you will cause to

be accompanied by these holy words: *"Joseph, nozo Maria, Yo te bautizo en el nombre del padre, y del hijo, y del espiritu-santo. Amen."*[45] And you should take great care that this statement is in the manner of Castile;[46] you are definitely not to say it in the manner of Mexico,[47] nor make up another word or mix in anything else in order to not spoil the baptism. With just this much it is fine, that is all to baptize the child as a priest would have baptized it. But because it can happen that no one is found who will know how to baptize in Spanish but only in Nahuatl, at that time let him baptize in Nahuatl so that it is possible for him to help his fellow man. However, it is certain that first he should get in the right frame of mind so that he can baptize if he can and to the extent that he can. Here are the holy words to baptize in Nahuatl and he should add nothing else at all to it: *"Josephê, nozo Mariaê, nehuatl nimitzquaatequia ica in itocatzin in tetâtzin, ihuan in tepiltzin, ihuan in espiritu-santo. Amèn."*[48]

And if the child cannot come out, he only really shows his hand or his foot, then at that time may the birthing woman be covered. And afterward, it will be good if a midwife or another woman baptizes the child on his hand or his foot if the woman knows how baptism is done, and if she does not know it, let whatever other knowledgeable person baptize him. And in the same way, first she should set her heart in order so that she can baptize if she can and to the extent she can. And afterward, she will pour the water on the child's hand or foot and accompany it with the holy words as already mentioned here. If it is not known whether the child is alive or has already died, then at that time first get in the right frame of mind so that you can baptize him/her if the child is alive. But on the contrary, you really must not baptize the child if he is already dead. And not until after you know should you pour water on him and pronounce the baptismal words in the manner already referred to.

45. "Joseph or María, I baptize you in the name of the Father and of the Son and of the Holy Spirit. Amen."

46. Spanish hereafter.

47. Nahuatl hereafter.

48. "Joseph or María, I baptize you in the name of the Father and the Son and the Holy Spirit. Amen." Paredes's reluctance for the baptizer to use Nahuatl represents a larger concern some ecclesiastics had regarding the ability of Nahuatl to accurately translate the baptismal words. See Christensen, *Nahua and Maya Catholicisms*, 155–56.

That is all that is needed for the baptism to be done correctly. And truly if the child dies, his parents should take him to the church and advise the priest how they baptized him so that likewise the child will be buried at the church. And if the child does not die, likewise they should take him to the church, and they should make it known to the priest how he was baptized so that he can consider what to do and so that he can finish everything that belongs to the baptism.

And concerning this, I very greatly implore all the Christian people for the sake of the divine blood of our lord Jesus Christ, let each person take care to learn and know by heart this baptism. And especially physicians, the healers, and the midwives should know it so that they can correctly perform (the baptism) when it is necessary. For that reason it is written here about how this baptism is to be correctly performed, so that everyone will know and be inspired to do it, and in case of necessity will carry it out. Because in that way we can greatly help children who are afflicted, and we will greatly please our God and our precious savior Jesus Christ.

4

Nahuatl and Maya Catechisms

It is known that many manners of doctrinas have already been composed in this land in the languages of the natives, primarily in the Mexican language [Nahuatl], which is the common [language], such as small or brief doctrinas from which children are taught, and other larger ones from which the adults and those more capable can understand the things of our Faith in full.
—*Códice franciscano*, 1570

Catechisms are books of Christian doctrine that outline the basic foundational tenets of the Faith. Often referred to as doctrinas, catechisms vary in content and length, although most include two sections: one contains various points of doctrine and prayers and the other a series of questions and answers representing a dialogue between a teacher and a student about the doctrine. The more lengthy versions could include exhaustive expositions of the doctrines and prayers and even instructions on how to perform everyday religious functions. Small catechisms were commonly intended for children and those considered neophytes in the Faith. These abbreviated manuals present the Christian doctrine in a simple, straightforward manner that omits much of the meatier content of their larger counterparts. The two manuals presented here are examples of this shorter, simplified version of Christianity.

Because catechisms served as a fundamental tool in evangelization, they were among the first works translated and printed in native languages in New Spain. In 1539 the bishop of Mexico, fray Juan de Zumárraga, ordered published the Nahuatl catechism *Breve y más compendiosa doctrina cristiana en lengua mexicana y castellana*. The necessity of creating texts that adequately conveyed the Catholic doctrine in Nahuatl inspired numerous other doctrinas such as those of the Dominican order (1548), fray Pedro de Gante (1553), and fray Domingo de la Anunciación (1565), among others. Many of these early publications included lengthy treatises and were produced during what has been called the classical age of Nahuatl, which lasted until the mid-seventeenth century.[1] Subsequent centuries, however, saw a decline in the publication of lengthy expositions of the Faith in Nahuatl, as ecclesiastics increasingly favored the production of shorter catechisms. From the mid-seventeenth century onward, brief catechisms frequently emerged from the printing presses of New Spain. Yet short catechisms in manuscript form were also common. These manuscripts primarily originated as works of independent authors not seeking publication or as copies of already existing printed catechisms. The two catechisms translated here are examples of the latter.

The general mid-seventeenth- and eighteenth-century trend among authors to favor a shorter Nahuatl catechism resulted for a variety of possible reasons. Recurring issues with unorthodoxy and questionable behavior curbed the initial optimism of friars who no doubt saw the lengthy catechism as a valuable tool in creating the ideal Nahua Christian. The decline of religious schools for the natives, such as the College of Tlatelolco, also created a shortage of demand and available trained natives to assist in text production.[2] As we have seen, this increasing shortage parallels the overall decline of the lengthy, eloquent religious texts evident in the sixteenth and early seventeenth century and the rise of shorter, simpler texts. Indeed, the general increase of errors and awkward phrasing from the mid-seventeenth century onward reflects this decline in native-ecclesiastic collaboration.[3] Furthermore, as the native population in central Mexico began to recover from its mid-seventeenth-century nadir and as evangelization continued to spread, ecclesiastics—who varied in their linguistic abilities—increasingly favored manuals that succinctly and efficiently taught the basic doctrine. The idea, as don Antonio Vázquez Gastelu's 1689 catechism stated, was to create a succinct catechism that contained "precisely that which the Christian should know."[4]

As mentioned earlier, the lack of a printing press combined with the limited number of ecclesiastics resulted in a dearth of printed works in Yucatan. That said, the importance of the catechism to

1. Sell, "Friars, Nahuas, and Books," 114–215.
2. Gibson, *The Aztecs*, 382–83.
3. Sousa, Poole, and Lockhart also suggest this in their *Story of Guadalupe*, 43–44.
4. Vázquez Gastelu, *Arte de lengua mexicana*, unnumbered. The phrase comes from the title of his catechism, a title he borrowed from Bartolomé Castaño's 1644 catechism, along with much of its content.

Yucatecan ecclesiastics is apparent when considering that among the first works in Maya was likely a catechism composed by fray Luis de Villalpando in the mid-sixteenth century. After Villalpando died in the 1550s, fray Diego de Landa produced a Maya catechism, but this too has gone missing. Various subsequent ecclesiastics composed Maya catechisms, but the first to survive and reach scholars today is fray Juan Coronel's 1620 *Doctrina*.[5]

All colonial catechisms in Maya extant today are relatively brief. At times, even these catechisms struggled to educate the Mayas— at least from the priest's point of view. Indeed, the priest of Yaxcabá complained in 1813 that "despite attending catechism daily . . . very many [Mayas] never learn it completely, even though the catechism is so brief that it can be recited in a quarter of an hour, more or less."[6] Overall, the number of Maya catechisms printed in the colonial period pales in comparison to those in Nahuatl, although surely many manuscript versions once existed.

Velázquez's Small Catechism (Nahuatl)

Carlos Celedonio Velázquez de Cárdenas y León included a brief discussion of the doctrine in his 1761 *Breve práctica y régimen del confessonario [sic] de indios en mexicano y castellano* to "easily enable [the natives] to achieve with certain probability the wholesome fruits of the holy sacraments."[7] Velázquez served as a professor of philosophy and vice rector of the Royal and Pontifical University of Mexico—one of the most important institutions for higher education in this period—and as the priest of the native parish of Otumba and its constituent *visitas*.[8] Velázquez designed his *Breve práctica* as an all-in-one manual for religious instruction and confession in Nahuatl. Today the work is rare, but a 1770 handwritten copy of the work by Manuel Joseph de Reyna survives in the Latin American

---

5. Tozzer, *Maya Grammar*, 196–97. For more information on Maya catechisms and Coronel's publications, see Hanks, *Converting Words*, 244–60.

6. Rugeley, *Maya Wars*, 29.

7. Velázquez, *Breve práctica*, 33.

8. *Visitas* were ancillary towns to principal towns, or *cabeceras*, that were occasionally visited by nonresident priests. José Mariano Beristáin de Souza claims that Velázquez was an Indian. *Biblioteca hispanoamericana septentrional*, 286.

Fig. 2 Joseph de Reyna's copy of Velázquez's catechism. TULAL R459, Latin American Library, Tulane University, New Orleans.

Library at Tulane (see fig. 2).[9] The catechism included in his work, and translated here, is a fairly close reproduction of the catechism of Bartolomé Castaño, a seventeenth-century Jesuit. During his ministry, which was located primarily in northern Mexico, Castaño developed a brief catechism, reportedly published in 1644, to convey the very basics of the Christian faith. The catechism saw various reprintings and was translated into a variety of languages.[10] In short, the catechism translated here provides an excellent example of what aspects of Catholicism an eighteenth-century ecclesiastic expected the priests to preach and the Nahuas to know.

9. Manuel Joseph de Reyna, "Este bocabulario lo hizo y cordino se su original el maestro Manuel Joseph de Reyna," 1770, Rare Miniature R459, Latin American Library, Tulane University, New Orleans. Joseph de Reyna curiously refers to the work as a "Vocabulario." Moreover, his copy is incomplete and omits the final pages of the 1761 original that detail how to administer the sacrament of extreme unction (last rites).

10. Castaño's brief Nahuatl catechism also appears in Ripalda, Catecismo mexicano, 143–50, and various other works. For more on Castaño's catechism and influence, see Burkhart, "Little Doctrine."

EXCERPT FROM *BREVE PRÁCTICA* (1761), COPIED
BY MANUEL JOSEPH DE REYNA (1770)

The doctrine in questions and answers arranged with brevity, following the mode of Father Castaño, and after the manner of many learned instructors that have taught it this way, for the most brief and easy instruction of the Indians.

Here is the questionnaire through holy words so that here in this way you will gradually learn what is your obligation concerning the Faith of our deity.

Q. Tell me, does the deity exist?
A. Yes, the deity, God, exists.
Q. How many deities are there?
A. Only one really true deity, God.
Q. Where is that deity, God?
A. He is there in heaven and here on earth and everywhere.
Q. Who made heaven and earth?
A. He, our lord God.
Q. Who is our lord God?
A. He is the Holy Trinity.
Q. Who is the Holy Trinity?
R. He is God the Father, and God his beloved child, and God the Holy Spirit, three divine persons, but one really true deity, God.
Q. Is the Father a deity?
A. Yes.
Q. Is the precious child of God a deity?
A. Yes.
Q. Is God the Holy Spirit a deity?
A. Yes.
Q. Are there three deities?
A. No, only one really true deity, God.[11]
Q. Who is the divine person that became a man?
A. He is the second of the persons, the precious revered child of God, our lord Jesus Christ.

---

11.   One of the greatest struggles ecclesiastics faced was explaining the Trinity to the natives while not encouraging their preexisting polytheistic views. For an excellent study, see Tavárez, "Naming the Trinity."

Q. Who is our lord Jesus Christ?

A. He is a really true deity, and a really true man.

Q. But from or with or by whom did our lord Jesus Christ become a man?

A. In the womb of the pure maiden, Holy Mary, the always really true virgin,[12] through a miracle of the Holy Spirit, and although she became the mother of our lord Jesus Christ, she never lost her precious maidenhood.

Q. But what is the reason our lord Jesus Christ became a man?

A. In order to redeem us sinners.

Q. What did he do here on earth when he came to redeem us?

A. He suffered for us during the reign of Pontius Pilate. His arms were spread out on the cross, he died, was buried, and descended to hell. On the third day he came to life on his own among the dead, he was raised to heaven, he went to sit on the right hand of God the Father, and from there he will come when Judgment Day is held, when he will come to judge the living and the dead.

Q. And who is the noblewoman, Holy Mary?

A. She is the precious honored mother of our deity; she is filled with perfect goodness, grace, and in her are all the various virtues in heaven and here on earth, and she is the universal queen everywhere.[13]

Q. Where is she, that eternal virgin noblewoman, Holy Mary?

A. She is in heaven; she has become our intercessor before our lord God, the Holy Trinity.

Q. Did our lord Jesus Christ die as a deity or as a man?

A. He did not die as a deity but only as a man.

Q. But when a human being of earth dies, does his soul die also as does his earthly body?

A. The soul does not die, only his earthly body.

Q. But does his body die forever?

A. No, when the Judgment Day is held, they (the soul and body) will unite again and will live forever.

---

12. This word derives from *ichpochtzintli*, which literally translates as "honored young maiden." In Nahua society an ichpochtli is an unmarried young woman. For more on this and other terms ascribed to the virgin Mary, see Sousa, Poole, and Lockhart, *Story of Guadalupe*, 39–41.

13. "Queen" is from *tlatocacihuapilli*, literally "ruler-noblewoman." Here, I follow the pattern established by Sousa, Poole, and Lockhart in translating the word as "queen." *Story of Guadalupe*, 40.

Q. And good souls, when they die where will they go?

A. They will go to heaven because they kept the holy command-ments of God and the Holy Church.

Q. And the bad souls, where will they go?

A. They will go to hell because they did not faithfully keep the holy commandments of God and the Holy Church.

Q. What does the "Holy Roman Catholic Church" mean?

A. It means the assembly of all Christians; our lord Jesus Christ is their head, and here on earth, his surrogate, our great priestly ruler, the Supreme Pontiff, who is in the great altepetl of Rome.

Q. And the angels, who are they?

A. They are beings of another order who sing joyously and in heaven are praising our lord God in song.

Q. Is this their only duty?

A. No, since our lord God chose them as our intercessors and our snatchers from the hands of others so that we will stay well within the divine commandments of our lord God, and when we are at the verge of death they will protect us from our enemies, the devils.

Q. Who is in the Holy Sacrament (the Eucharist)?

A. Our lord Jesus Christ, the really true deity and really true man, is there; as he is in heaven, similarly, he is in the host, inside the chalice, and in each little part.

Q. And what does a Christian do to receive well the Holy Sacrament?

A. He will receive it through fasting and through confession if there is some mortal sin upon his soul.

Q. And what does a Christian do to confess well?

A. First, he will search his mind and remember so that he declares, relates well all his sins; he will hide nothing, nothing will he leave out for shame, he will clearly relate everything and never again will he sin; he will feel bad, anxious, because he offended our deity; he will receive and perform whatever penance our confessor orders him (to carry out).

A Methodist Catechism (Maya)

Catholics were not the only ones who produced catechisms in Mesoamerica. After Mexico gained its independence from Catholic Spain in 1821, liberalism and its censorship of Catholicism officially opened the door for Protestant missionaries with the Constitution of 1857, which implicitly legalized Protestantism. Yet even prior to the region's independence from Spain, Mesoamerica had caught the eye of Protestant missionaries, and the Yucatan provided a foothold. Since the middle of the seventeenth century, British pirates and loggers had settled on the eastern border of the Yucatan Peninsula in British Honduras, or what today is Belize. As a British-populated settlement, Belize provided a home to some of the earliest Protestant missionaries. Scottish Presbyterians arrived in the 1820s, Baptist missionaries in 1822, and Wesleyan Methodist missionaries in 1825.[14] Among the latter was Richard Fletcher.

After wetting his feet on the West African coast in Sierra Leone, and still fueled with the missionary zeal characteristic of eighteenth- and nineteenth-century Protestantism, Fletcher received his appointment to Belize in 1855. Prior to Fletcher's arrival, the Wesleyan Methodist missionaries had struggled, with limited success. The first ten years of evangelization produced only 110 society members, and a 1905 census counted only 308 Protestants in Yucatan.[15] Due to illness, most missionaries returned to London shortly after their arrival and thus did not stay long enough to adequately learn Spanish, let alone Maya. The recent outbreak of the Caste War in 1847 had funneled refugees, including Mayas, into Belize. By 1861 an estimated thirteen thousand speakers of Yucatec Maya resided in the colony.[16] Fletcher dedicated his first years in Belize to learning Spanish and Maya, and by the end of his twenty-five year stay—much of it in the border town of Corozal—published a translation of three of the Gospels, a book of prayers, and a catechism, all in Yucatec Maya.[17] Throughout his ministry Fletcher traveled widely and eventually gained permission from the governor of Yucatan in 1871 to preach Methodism. In fact, the governor expressed an interest in obtaining any religious tract composed in Maya that Fletcher could provide. This only encouraged the missionary, who had great hopes

---

14. Findlay and Holdsworth, *History*, 2:291; Bristowe and Wright, *Handbook of British Honduras*, 149.

15. Johnson, *Christianity in Belize*, 168; Baldwin, *Mexican Revolution*, 60.

16. Rugeley, *Maya Wars*, 104. For an excellent study on the Caste War, see Rugeley's *Yucatán's Maya Peasantry*.

17. The only other known producers of Protestant Maya religious texts are Alexander Henderson and John Kingdon, both Baptist missionaries. See Tozzer, *Maya Grammar*, 145–46, 237.

for Methodism's future in Yucatan. But natural disasters, a decline in the local trade, and disease took a heavy toll on the Methodist's efforts, and when disease compelled Fletcher to leave Belize in 1880, he left a struggling ministry.[18]

Fletcher is almost certainly the author of a Methodist Spanish-Maya catechism published in London in 1865 and intended for young children, titled *Catecismo de los metodistas. No. 1, para los niños de tierna edad. Catecismo ti le metodistaoob. No. 1, utial mehen palaloob.*[19] The catechisms employed by the nineteenth-century Wesleyan Methodists included one titled *Catechisms of the Wesleyan Methodists . . . No. 1, for Children of Tender Years,* and the 1865 Spanish-Maya catechism follows contemporary editions of this work very closely.[20] A letter written by Fletcher in 1863 indicates that he employed the help of others—likely Maya assistants—in composing his translation: "I have translated into Maya, with the best help I can get, the First Catechism."[21] The Maya catechism translated here is an anonymous manuscript copy of the 1865 printed work (see fig. 3).[22] But the manuscript catechism is incomplete and fails to finish recording the final pages of the published catechism.[23] To provide the reader with the entire translation, I employ the 1865 work to complete the final part.

Catholic and Methodist catechisms share some general similarities, but each reflects the individual emphases of each tradition. Generally speaking, colonial Catholicism emphasized its seven sacraments, although all were not essential for salvation. To educate

18. For a general history of Fletcher's experience in Belize, see Findlay and Holdsworth, *History,* 2:432–40.

19. Although the work is anonymous, Fletcher's role as author is all but agreed on by scholars. See Tozzer, *Maya Grammar,* 197.

20. For one comparative example, see *Catechisms.*

21. *Wesleyan Missionary Notices,* 171.

22. The oscillation between Spanish and Maya sections in the manuscript aligns perfectly with the Spanish and Maya columns and page interruptions of the printed work.

23. William Gates acquired the manuscript and in 1930 sold it to Robert Garrett, who eventually donated it to Princeton University. Unfortunately, the manuscript fails to provide any information on the identity of its author, provenance, or date. Although the orthography and the document itself betray its late nineteenth-century origin, we are left to speculate as to the author's identity. After a few blank pages, a new work begins with the heading *"Conosimiento y virtudes de las yerbas Yucatecas estractadas del manuscrito que dejo D. Ricardo Osada—alias el Judio"* (Knowledge and benefits of the Yucatecan herbs taken from the manuscript left by D. Ricardo Osada—the "Jew").

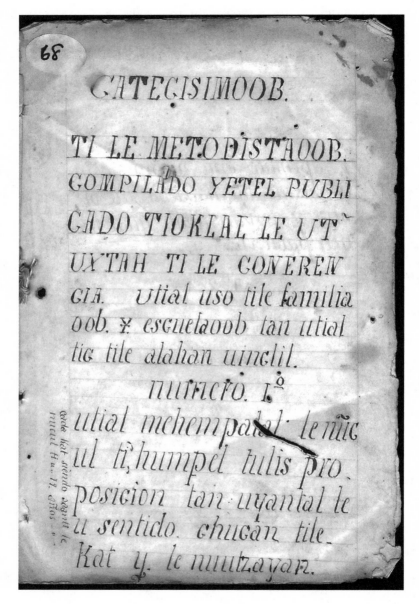

Fig. 3 Catecisimoob ti le metodistaoob. Garrett-Gates Mesoamerican Manuscripts, no. 68. Manuscripts Division, Department of Rare Books and Special Collections, Princeton University Library.

its followers on the doctrines necessary for the correct performance and understanding of such sacraments, particularly confession, the church stressed additional core doctrines and devotions such as the Decalogue, Articles of Faith, Commandments of the Church, and the seven mortal sins and virtues. Finally, select prayers, including the Sign of the Cross, the Lord's Prayer, the Hail Mary, the Apostles' Creed, and the Salve Regina, also played a fundamental role in the church's catechesis.

The vast majority of Catholic catechisms produced in colonial Mexico and Yucatan convey these points of doctrine and practice. Even abbreviated catechisms contain such fundamental doctrine. Indeed, prior to Velázquez's questions-and-answers portion of the catechism, he included Nahuatl translations of the Sign of the Cross, Act of Contrition, the Lord's Prayer, the Hail Mary, the Apostles' Creed, the Salve Regina, the Decalogue, the Commandments of the Church, the sacraments, Articles of Faith, and a prayer for the suffering souls in purgatory, called a *sudario* in reference to the burial shroud of Christ. Many such points of doctrine were again treated in the questions and answers of his catechism.

Methodism, like many other movements within Protestantism, emphasized the importance of personal conversion, the authority of the Bible, and an education established on biblical teachings through schools and colleges. The authority of the Bible was such that all doctrine not supported by biblical evidence was considered anathema: "The Holy Scriptures contain everything necessary to salvation: so that whatsoever is not read therein, nor may be proved thereby, is not to be required of any man, that it should be believed as an article of faith, or be thought requisite or necessary for salvation."[24] For example, since the New Testament Christ mentions specifically and commands adherence to only two sacraments—baptism and communion—these are the only ones that came to be adopted by the Methodists, a tradition they inherited from Protestantism in general.[25] Confession, a topic covered at length in nearly every Catholic catechism, fails to appear in Methodist counterparts, which hold repentance at an individual level without the need for absolution from a priest. The role of grace apart from works in salvation is also

24. *Doctrines and Disciplines*, 7. See also Roeber, "Waters of Rebirth," 74.
25. *Doctrines and Disciplines*, 11.

emphasized throughout. Moreover, whereas the second commandment in the Catholic Decalogue prohibits the taking of the Lord's
name in vain, the Methodists, like many Protestants, given a long-
standing difference in numbering the commandments within Christianity, use the second commandment to emphasize the prohibition
of making or worshiping any "graven images." Finally, there is a
noticeable emphasis in the Methodist catechisms on biblical history.

Although designed for small children, the Maya Methodist catechism examined here reflects such topics, and much of its material
stresses an understanding of the biblical doctrine and how people,
although born proud and loving themselves, can achieve salvation only
by accepting Christ through repentance validated by the Holy Spirit.
Other nineteenth-century Methodist catechisms intended for more
mature audiences detail the necessity of baptism and communion,
the importance of the Bible and prayer, and more details on the death
and judgment that will occur during the Second Coming. In addition,
Methodism's emphasis on the individual experience of religion comes
through in the subtitle of the Maya manuscript catechism that identi-
fies its designated audience as "families and schools."[26] This too, inherited from Luther and the Protestant tradition in general, emphasized
that ministers did not monopolize the role of education but shared
their pedagogical roles with fathers and, secondarily, mothers, who
were responsible for inculcating the catechism in their children. Lastly,
the manuscript catechism further reflects Methodism's emphasis on
the Bible through its proposed appendix that was to contain a catechistic survey of biblical characters and prayers. Although the title page
of the manuscript describes this appendix and it appears in the 1865
printed work, it is absent from the manuscript text.

CATECISIMOOB TI LE METODISTAOOB (1860S–1900), FOLS. 1V–7R,
AND *CATECISMO DE LOS METODISTAS* (1865), 7–10

Catechisms of the Methodists. Compiled and published by the order
of the conference for the use of the families and schools related to the
mentioned body (Methodists).[27]

26. This designation is also present in other nineteenth-century editions of the
catechism.
27. Although the catechism appears in both Maya and Spanish, my English
translation derives solely from the Maya. *Catecisimoob ti le metodistaoob*, Princeton
University Library, Garrett-Gates Mesoamerican Manuscripts, no. 68.

Number 1

For small children; the response to each question being given by way
of one entire proposal whose meaning comes forth here compiled
in the questions and answers that follow. With an appendix, where
there is a short catechism of biblical names and prayers for small
children.

A. 2[28]

(*From the heart*)[29]

First Catechism

Section 1, God

1. Question. Tell me, small child, who made you?

Answer. God made me.

Q. Who is God?

A. God is the infinite and eternal spirit that is before, that is today,
that is without end.

Q. Where is God?

A. God is everywhere.

Q. What can God do?

A. God can do whatever he desires.

Q. Does God know all things?

A. God knows all that is in a person's mind, his heart, everything he
says, and all his works.

Q. Will he call us to remember the account of all the things we think
and do?

A. God will call us in order to give an account of everything we think
and do because the Final Judgment will bring judgment for all works
and all secret things, whether good or bad.

Q. Does God love you?

A. God loves all things he made.

Q. What did God make?

A. All things, especially the righteous man.

Section 2, How man was made

Q. How did God make man?

A. God made the body of man with the dust of the earth.

[Q.] Did his soul come from the dust?

28. "A. 2" is a reference to the page number as it appears in the printed work.
29. This phrase does not appear in the printed work.

A. The soul of man did not come from the dust because God blew in his nose the breath of life; then there was a man with a living soul.

Q. Why was man made?

A. So that we can know and love and be happy with him (God) forever.

Q. Where did God place the first man and first woman?

A. The first man and first woman were placed by God in paradise.

Q. Man was made similar to whom?

A. Man was made similar to God by way of knowledge, holiness, happiness, and never dying (immortality).[30]

Section 3, Relating the fall of man

Q. [Did] those, our first parents, remain good and holy?

A. Those, our first parents, did not remain good and holy because they sinned against God; they fell into misery.

Q. What is sin?

A. Everything is sin.[31]

Q. What law did God give to our first parents in paradise?

A. The law God gave to our first parents in paradise was that he told them not to eat of the fruit of the tree given the name of knowledge of good and evil.

Q. [Did] they obey that which was said to them?

A. They did not obey what was said to them because they ate of the fruit of the tree.

Q. What evil came upon them because they ate it?

A. The evil that came upon them because they ate the fruit of the tree was that they were caused to leave paradise. Then they left for another, evil land of pain and death.

Q. [Did] their sin make ruin upon others besides themselves?

A. Their sin made ruin upon all persons on this earth.

Q. How were they ruined?

A. The first sin of our parents made ruin for all men by making them be born in sin; thus only evil is in their hearts and they can think only evil things, and they remain having pain and death.

---

30. This is the answer to the subsequent question, which the scribe either intentionally or unintentionally skipped, that asks how man was made similar to God.

31. This line differs from the Maya in the 1865 work, which carries the more accurate meaning that any transgression of the law of God is a sin.

Q. How are people born in sin?

A. All persons are born in sin because they are born prideful, they do not listen (obstinate), they are lovers of things on this earth and not of God.

Section 4, Of the redemption of man

Q. Because of whom are we saved from sin?

A. We are saved from sin because of Jesus Christ, the eternal son of God.

Q. What did Jesus Christ do to save us?

A. Jesus Christ was made man, honorably suffered death for us, was resurrected among the dead, and rose to heaven; this only in order to save us.

Q. What can we gain from his becoming man for us, and his death for us?

A. [From] his becoming man and dying for us, we receive forgiveness of sins, holiness, and eternal happiness in heaven.

Q. But will he save all people?

A. Christ saves only those that repent themselves and that believe in him, etc.

Q. What thing is it to repent?

A. To repent is for people to have pain for their sins, to confess and forsake them, and to seek the forgiveness of God.

Q. What is it to believe in Jesus Christ?

A. They that believe in Jesus Christ receive his words, and they trust only in those merits of his death for salvation.

Q. Are you able to do all these things alone?

A. No, I cannot repent by myself, nor believe by myself, but God will help me by his Holy Spirit if I ask him.

Q. What will happen to those that do not repent nor abandon their sins and do not believe in Jesus Christ nor hear his word?

A. Those that do not repent nor abandon their sins and do not believe in Jesus Christ, those that die will be thrown into hell.

Section 5, Of heaven and hell

Q. What is hell?

A. Hell is a very dark well of never-ending depth full of fire and sulfur.

Q. How will the wicked be punished there?

A. The wicked will be punished in hell by the wounding of their bodies with fire, and their souls by suffering the wrath of God.

Q. When will this state of pain end?

A. This state of pain in hell will slowly last forever.

Q. Where will those that believe be after they die?

A. After they die, those that believe will go to heaven.

Q.[32] What thing is heaven?

A. Heaven is a place where there is light and glory.

Q. How will the righteous live there?

A. The righteous will live in heaven with their joy and happiness forever.

Q. Never will they suffer anything?

A. The righteous will never suffer anything in heaven since they never will have need, nor pain, nor sin.

Q. What form of bodies will they have?

A. The righteous in heaven will have bodies that will never die made just like the glorified body of our lord Jesus Christ.

Q. How will they use them?

A. The righteous in heaven will use them in order to praise and serve God, and [in] works of love to one as the other.

[Section 6, Of our duty to God and man][33]

Q. What type of person is it necessary for you to become so that you will go to that glorious and good place?

A. In order to go to this glorious and good place, I have to make myself holy in heart and in life.

Q. What does it mean to be holy in heart?

A. To be holy in heart means freedom from anger, pride, love of the world, and all other sins and to love the lord God with all my heart and all my understanding, and all my soul, and all my strength.

Q. What does it mean to be holy in life?

A. The holy life [means] I fulfill my duty to God and to mankind as says the holy word of God.

Q. What is your duty to God?

---

32. Here begins the translation from [Fletcher], *Catecismo de los metodistas*, 7–10.

33. This and the subsequent section appear together under section 5 in the printed work. I have included them here for convenience and to reflect the common practice of Methodist catechisms at the time.

A. My duty to God [is that] I heed his word, his laws; I honor and worship him.

Q. What is your duty to mankind?

A. My duty to mankind [is that] I heed the words of my parents, that I honor my superiors, I always speak the truth, and that I am just, mild, and charitable to all.

Q. How can you do this thing?

A. I can fulfill my duty to God and to mankind only through the grace of God.

Q. What is this grace of God?

A. The grace of God is the strength of the Holy Spirit that we have in order to believe, love, and serve God.

Q. How should we find this grace?

A. We should find this grace of God in the tireless and diligent use of the means of grace.

Q. Which are the first means of grace?

A. The first means of grace are prayer in secret and also with all the righteous, the reading of the Bible, the hearing the word of God preached, the holy Eucharist, and the fast.

Q. How much time should all Christians use the means of grace?

A. All Christians should use the means of grace until the end of his life.

[Section 7, The Lord's Prayer, Creed, and Ten Commandments]

Q. Recite the Our Father (the Lord's Prayer).

A. Our father, you are in heaven, blessed is your name, your kingdom comes for us, your will be done on earth as in heaven. Give us this day our bread of today, and forgive us our trespasses as we forgive those that trespass against us. And do not leave us to fall in temptation, but free us from evil. For yours is the kingdom, the power, and the glory without end.

Q. Recite the things that you believe (the Apostles' Creed).

A. I believe in God the Father Almighty, creator of heaven and earth, and also Jesus Christ, the only son of our lord who was conceived by the Holy Spirit, born of Virgin Mary, suffered under the power of Pontius Pilate, then was crucified, died, and was buried; he descended to hell; on the third day again he lived (resurrected) among the dead; he ascended to heaven and is seated on the right hand of God the Father Almighty; from there he will come to judge the living and the dead. I believe in the Holy Spirit, the holy universal church, the communion of the saints, the forgiveness of sins, the living again (resurrection) of the body, and life without end (everlasting).

Q. Recite the Ten Commandments.

A. God spoke all these words, saying,

1. I am Jehovah your God; I removed you from the land of Egypt, from the house of labor; you will not have other gods before me.

2. [You] will not make images nor any [likeness][34] of things in heaven, nor below on the earth, nor in the water under the earth. You will not bow down to them, nor will you honor them, because I am Jehovah your God, strong, jealous; I [visit][35] the wickedness of the fathers on the children of the third and fourth generations of those that hate me. And I prepare mercy for all that love me and that keep my commandments.

3. You will not use the name Jehovah your God in vain because Jehovah God will not consider innocent those that use his name in vain.

4. You will remember the Sabbath day to sanctify it. Six days you will labor and perform your work, but the seventh day is the Sabbath of Jehovah your God. You will not do any work, nor your son, nor your daughter, nor your servant, nor your animals, nor the stranger [that is within your doors],[36] because in six days Jehovah God made the heaven and the earth, the sea, and all things that are in them, and on the seventh day he rested. Thus Jehovah blessed the Sabbath day and sanctified it.

5. Honor your father and your mother so that your days are prolonged in the land that Jehovah your God gives [you].

6. You will not kill.

7. You will not commit adultery.

8. You will not steal.

9. You will not speak against your neighbor if it is not true.

10. You will not covet the house of your neighbor; you will not covet the wife of your neighbor, nor his man-servant, nor his maidservant, nor his cow, nor his ass, nor anything belonging to your neighbor. (Exodus 10: 1–17)

34. Illegible. Translation from the Spanish version.
35. Illegible. Translation from the Spanish version.
36. Illegible. Translation from the Spanish version.

5

Experience teaches me that using this [confessional manual] always results in very consoled penitents and a satisfied priest, who always longs for the true fruit of the sacrament of penance.
—Carlos Celedonio Velázquez de Cárdenas y León, *Breve práctica*, 1761

The sacrament of penance provides Catholics with a means to repent of sins committed after baptism. Confession, or the act of confessing one's sins, is an important part of the sacrament that evolved over time from a public, infrequent experience to a more private and periodic occurrence by the sixteenth century.[1] Because the sin, motive, and remorse of a sinner became increasingly important, and due to the mandate of the Fourth Lateran Council in 1215 for an annual confession, confessional manuals emerged as early as the thirteenth century to help guide the priest and penitent through a successful confession. These manuals typically included preconfessional speeches and questions designed to aid penitents to remember and feel sorrow for their sins, followed by the confessional questions themselves structured around the Ten Commandments, the five commandments of the church, the fourteen works of mercy, the five senses, the seven deadly sins, and the seven virtues.

Confessional manuals followed European ecclesiastics as they crossed the Atlantic and began evangelizing the Nahuas and Mayas. The majority of manuals composed in central Mexico and Yucatan were polyglot works in that their contents appeared in both Spanish and the native language. This increased the ability of ecclesiastics unfamiliar with native languages to confess natives. In addition, the manuals allowed literate natives to prepare themselves for confession by illustrating what questions would be asked and what was expected of them. Similar to their European predecessors, the questions of Nahua and Maya confessional manuals were tailored to address the

1. Homza, "European Link."

ailments of the penitent. As such, they contained not only standard questions inquiring after belief in the Faith, but also those local topics that particularly concerned ecclesiastics, such as idolatry and drunkenness.[2]

Like other native-language religious texts, confessional manuals changed over the course of the colonial period. Sixteenth-century Nahuatl manuals either were standard length or appeared as "small" and "large" versions, *confesionario breve* and *mayor*. Large manuals often included lengthy introductory speeches detailing the intricacies necessary for the ideal confession, along with many pages of questions that probed the innermost corners of the natives' lives. In reality, and similar to their European counterparts, these large manuals were intended for personal reference and study, and many were printed alongside shortened versions designed for the confessional. Unlike their larger counterparts, small manuals generally limited their contents to the basic questions deemed necessary for the penitent.

Fray Alonso de Molina's sixteenth-century Spanish and Nahuatl *Confessionario mayor* and *Confessionario breve* provide an illustrative example (see fig. 4). Although Molina published both works together, they differ in content. The prologue to the large manual contains thirty-two pages of admonitory text intended to educate sinners on what, why, and how they should confess and to motivate them to feel sorrow and remorse for their sins. This chapter includes a translation of this text. These preconfessional admonitions again illustrate the elegant, descriptive prose tailored to Nahua rhetoric that resulted from friars' early collaboration with natives—Molina was known to have collaborated with the Nahua Hernando de Ribas on various projects. Furthermore, the speeches demonstrate the Franciscan's general enthusiasm for and expectations of the Nahuas in the early colonial period. Such enthusiasm also is reflected in the hundreds of questions that follow, but I will spare the reader those translations. In contrast, Molina's small manual barely has any admonitory speeches and contains roughly half the questions.

---

2. For more on the ability of confessional manuals to betray cultural insights, see Christensen, *Nahua and Maya Catholicisms*, 159–92, and Barnes, "Catechisms and Confessionarios." For more on the ecclesiastics' concern with drunkenness, see Corcuera de Mancera, *Fraile*.

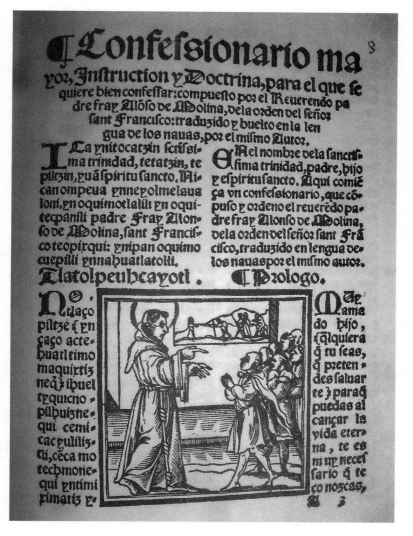

Fig. 4 Fray Alonso de Molina's 1569 *Confessionario mayor*, fol. 3r.

Like many of his European predecessors, Molina wrote both his large and small manuals for specific purposes. He stated that he designed his large manual for literate Nahuas and ecclesiastics; the former to educate them on sin and how to confess, the latter to help them better understand their Nahua penitents and assist them in preaching the Gospel. His small manual, however, was meant specifically for the confession itself, although surely confessors, when necessary and as was customary, could refer to the large manual for additional questions on a particular sin.[3] Thus, the selected text from Molina's large manual translated here was intended for the personal study and reference of both Nahuas and ecclesiastics.

Eventually, the publication of large Nahuatl confessional manuals generally followed the decline of large catechisms, and by the mid-seventeenth century they ceased to appear on the printing presses of central Mexico. Arguably for similar reasons, including the generally tempered expectations for natives, the decline and limits of schools encouraging Nahuatl text production, and the challenge of managing an expanding evangelization program to care for a growing native population, ecclesiastics—particularly those struggling with the native language—increasingly favored small manuals.[4] Seventeenth- and eighteenth-century small manuals in Nahuatl commonly appeared in increasingly abbreviated forms with streamlined questions that addressed only the most relevant sins deemed common among natives living in a specific region and era.

This streamlined confession becomes vividly apparent in a Nahuatl manual published in Velázquez's 1761 *Breve práctica*. Absent are the lengthy, admonitory, preconfessional speeches like those found in Molina's large manual. Instead, immediately after his small confessional manual, Velázquez inserted a treatise in Nahuatl that he petitioned all ministers of native parishes to read to their Nahua fold before administering a high mass. The treatise clarifies for Nahuas what is and what is not a sin. This is not only to help natives avoid various sins, but also to assist in acquiring a better, more efficient confession by preventing Nahuas from confessing unnecessary sins and thus wasting time. In the process the text unintentionally provides a view of the daily religious life for a wide variety of Nahuas in central Mexico. This chapter includes a translation of this treatise. Compared to Molina's admonitions, Velázquez's text presents expectations

3. Molina, *Confesionario mayor*, 2v, 6v.

4. For insights on the eighteenth-century priests' view of the natives, see Taylor, *Magistrates of the Sacred*, 173–77. Many small Nahuatl confessional manuals accommodated those priests novice in the language and experience. For example, see Velázquez, *Breve práctica*, 1–16, which provides priests with, among other things, a lesson on numerical and kinship vocabulary in Nahuatl.

alleviated somewhat by more than two hundred years of negotiations between prescribed and practiced Christianity in central Mexico and the overall increasingly apparent desire to simplify the confession.

Finally, this chapter provides an example of a small confessional manual with its translation of fray Juan Coronel's 1620 Maya manual.[5] As mentioned, since the beginning of the colonial period Yucatan received limited numbers of ecclesiastics. These ecclesiastics seemed to have immediately embraced the small confessional manual; to my knowledge no large manual in Maya ever left the printing presses. The first evidence of a Maya confessional manual extant today is found in Coronel's 1620 *Discursos predicables,* and it is a small manual. Coronel's manual includes a few brief admonitory speeches at the end, yet its questions are terse and to the point. In fact, Coronel suggests at the beginning of the confession that the manual's general questions are to be employed only if the Maya penitent has not come prepared to confess his sins. To be sure, the manual aptly represents the simplified structure needed for confession in Yucatan and joins Molina's admonitory speech and Velázquez's treatise to provide a rare glimpse of confessional manuals and their variety and transformation.

Excerpt from Fray Alonso de Molina,
Confessionario mayor (1569), fols. 3r–19v

Large guide to confession, instruction, and doctrine for those who wish to confess well: composed by the reverend father fray Alonso de Molina, of the order of Saint Francis. Translated and done in the language of the Nahuas, by the same author.

In the name of the most holy Trinity, the Father, the Son, and the Holy Spirit, here sets forth a confessional manual, composed

5. Because Coronel's manual is surely the most accessible confessional manual in Maya, it has warranted the attention of various scholars. René Acuña included it in his 1998 reprint of Coronel's *Arte.* David Bolles produced a wonderful PDF transcription of the entire *Discursos predicables,* accessible on the FAMSI website, which has proved most helpful for this project. John Chuchiak provided an English translation of the section on the sixth commandment concerning fornication in his "Secrets Behind the Screens," 89–90. And Hanks's *Converting Words,* 263–62, provides an English translation of a few select questions. Mine, however, is the first English translation of the entire manual, although my translation does not include the few speeches and vocabulary list of kinship terms that follow the confession.

and arranged by father fray Alonso de Molina, Franciscan friar, who translated it into Nahuatl.

Prologue

My beloved child, whoever you are, who wants to be saved, so that you can achieve eternal life, it is very necessary for you to know yourself and remember you are a sinner before our lord. It is written in the Holy Scriptures: *Seven times a day the just will fall.*[6] It means a person of good life, whose deeds are just, falls and sins seven times a day. And although this is understood concerning small, venial sins that because of which our lord's grace is not lost, nevertheless through this we are told that we are all sinners and make mistakes in many things. As Saint James says: *We all offend in many things.*[7] It means in very many things we sin and we err. These divine words are understood to apply to the just, who cannot free themselves of little sins while living on earth. How much more will it apply to the great sinners who have fallen into very many kinds of mortal sins, they who have gone about committing every evil, who have often tripped? They fell into a hole of sin so that they were thrown down to hell.

Because of this, you sinner, you will say before our lord, as the wise man said, "He who confesses his sin before his deity, his ruler, would say, 'My lord! I cannot consider myself pure before you. Not in the slightest can I say that my heart is clean. Nor can I say I have no sin, and I know that no one else of all who live on the earth can say it because no one can with truth consider himself good before you.'"[8] If someone should say, "I have no sin,"[9] he is very deceived and he does not say the truth,[10] because we are all sinners and we have a great need for penance,[11] as said your precious disciple Saint Paul. He who does not acknowledge himself a sinner, who thinks he has nothing to worry about, to cry and be sad about, that he has no need for penance, one who is this way is exceedingly confused; there is nothing at all as lamentable, because that which is not understood

---

6. Original in Latin. In the column is "Pro. 24" (Prov. 24).
7. Original in Latin. In the column is "Iacob. 3." (James 3).
8. In the column is "p. 18 24" (Prov. 18:24)
9. In the column is "Prou. 20" (Prov. 20).
10. In the column is "1. Ioan. 1" (1 John 1).
11. In the column is "Roma. 3." (Rom. 3).

as sin, and the evil that is not seen as evil, are exceedingly dangerous and deprive people of sense.

Therefore, it is very necessary for you to recognize that you are a sinner if you want mercy bestowed upon you. Tell me, my precious child! If you hide your sore that makes you very sick, how will the healer heal you? How will he apply his medicine in order to mitigate your torment, your pain? It will be entirely impossible for you to recover your health. You will only worsen, and your suffering, your torment, your pain will only grow. On account of this, it is very necessary for you to understand that this is the foundation of your salvation: the knowledge of your sins; and knowledge of your sins, by which you confess and acknowledge your wickedness so that you see yourself as nothing, is also the beginning and foundation of the knowledge of divine wisdom. And knowledge of our lord also begins with fear of him.

These two things, knowledge of sin and fear of God, begin with the concern over sin with which your heart is afflicted because of your sins, because you offended him, your deity and ruler, so that you greatly weep and grieve, and this way from your emotional pain and concern emerges your confession, by which you declare and express all your wickedness before a priest—our lord God's representative. Whereupon you make restitution, you replace all that is necessary for you to replace. You satisfy others, return to people their property and their honor. Through penance you make restitution and make up for all your sins.

And when you have performed these three things relating to your penance, thereupon you will placate your deity and ruler concerning each of the things in which you have offended him. You will become his precious friend. He will take you as a child, and you will take him as a father. Because of this, it is very necessary for you to first know what is inside is your soul, which does not appear on the outside, so that later you should be worthy of knowing the difficult, marvelous, and very delightful things that pertain to our lord God. If you are not worthy to first know how you are, if you cannot first see yourself, you will not deserve to see and know the one God, you cannot know him with the vision of your soul, for he is especially seen when you have first seen and known yourself. For Saint Bernard says to you, know yourself so that you may become very famed and honored![12]

12. In the column is "Bernar." (St. Bernard).

The better way for you to become famed and honored is not if you know how the heavens rotate and how the stars are situated and in what manner our lord God placed usefulness to people in all the herbs and roots and what is the nature of the animals with four legs, even if you know how things are in the heavens and everywhere on earth, if you do not know yourself, do not see yourself as you are. For there are many alive who know very many things, but they do not know themselves, and true proper wisdom, called Philosophy, is knowledge of oneself.

Now, it is also very necessary for you to remember what is said in the Holy Scriptures: *Who knows his own sins?*[13] It means who fully knows and understands his own sins, his wickedness? It is as though the prophet means no one whosoever can fully know and understand each of the sins with which he has offended his deity and ruler, because then the prophet said: *The many things that are hiding my sins.*[14] It means, "O lord God! Help me with all my sins that are hidden, that I cannot remember, and those that I do not recognize as sins."

Now consider how very necessary it is for you to remember and know your sins in order that you can be saved! Not only is it necessary to recognize and remember them, it is also in addition very necessary for you to confess before a priest when our mother, the Holy Church, commands.

For this reason, I thought I would write for you these two confessional manuals as reminders. The first is rather long. It is necessary for you in order for me to help you a bit concerning your salvation; you Christian who has dedicated yourself to our savior Jesus Christ, who is already a believer in him and holds the holy Catholic faith. And the second, small confessional manual will belong to your confessor for the purpose of him being able to understand your Nahuatl speech or language. The first confessional manual that belongs to you is especially and exceedingly necessary for you, so that your soul will be eternally enriched and happy through our lord God, in whom I have great hope that he will help me with his very marvelous grace so that here you will see and read how you are to seek and recognize your sins that put you in danger and afflict you greatly and how to

13. Original in Latin. In the column is "Psalm 18" (Ps. 18).
14. Original in Latin.

relate all and be able to acknowledge it before a priest when you confess so that through your confession you will again achieve and make manifest the purity and goodness of your soul and all of the gifts of our lord God that you were given when you were baptized with God's water but that through your sins you lost. So that you will again attain it and see it, it is necessary for you to perform penance; since only because of it alone will you be able to become pure again and attain all of the goodness you lost through your sins.

Because of this, here I will first declare to you how very necessary it is for you to confess; then I will inform you of all, however many, the things necessary for you to do in order to seek out your sins and how you are to weep over them. Afterward, I will go along interrogating you on the divine Ten Commandments and the five commandments of the Holy Church. Also, I will ask you about the seven deadly sins, and also I will ask you about the seven mercies that pertain to our flesh, and the other seven that pertain to our soul. And I will ask you about our five senses and about our souls' potential. Also, I will ask you about the purifying theological and cardinal virtues. Afterward, at the end, I will make a speech for you so that you will thank your deity and ruler when you have confessed.

Here is that which the priest will advise him/her who is about to confess so that he/she will confess well, so that he/she will be well aware of all the things associated with his/her confession.

Now listen my precious child who has come to tell me your sins, to confess before our lord God and before me, his representative. You have come to help your soul and save it from hell, and through your confession you have come to attain eternal life, and our creator and benefactor, God, wants to be merciful to you, he wants to have compassion on you so that you will not perish forever, for he does not want one who voluntarily wants to come to his senses, who wants to change his life, who is determined never to sin again, to go to hell. In order that he can have compassion on you and so that you can placate him, also in order that he can cleanse you of your sins since your soul is corrupted and as though blackened, it is necessary that you do three things.

First, it is very necessary for you to prepare first and remember well and seek out all your sins and for those you have remembered to make you weep greatly as did ruler Hezekiah, who said to our lord God, "Our lord, ruler! With my soul's tears and sadness I will remember all the years I lived here on earth."[15] And not just once did he do this, but very often he would set himself to thinking about all his sins with which he offended God, concerning all the years that he lived here on earth. And it is very necessary for you to do it too so that you confess well. It is your great obligation that you examine yourself and remember all your mortal sins so that not a single one will you forget. And it is your obligation that they inflict anguish upon you and you will be repentant of them before your deity, your ruler, God, so that afterward you will confess. And you should examine yourself well so that all your sins you will remember well, and you should make every effort so that your penance will not be spoiled.

You should follow the example of the *mayordomo*[16] when his ruler is about to examine him. When he is beginning to examine him concerning his stewardship, then already he will relate how he made expenditures and where he assigned all the property that he was entrusted with. He takes great trouble to seek out and remember all the property that was given to him and where it went and was used so that he will satisfy his lord and so he will not be accused of anything, nor be ashamed or be belittled from misuse of property so that they will not falsely accuse him of being a thief, and he is very frightened and fears his punishment.

In the same fashion it is necessary for you to take great trouble and make every effort to seek out and remember all your sins so that you confess well, so that you will give account before our lord God and before a priest so that you will not be shamed or punished, but you will be honored and save your soul. If you do not first remember to gather together your sins, certainly for that reason you will spoil your confession, nor will it help your soul, but you will especially suffer for it.[17] Your confession will not help you but will become the reason for your being shamed, despised, and entirely condemned. So that you will not spoil it, first entirely of your own will seek out and gather all your sins. Remember well all the things worthy of remembering that I place before you here!

---

15. In the column is "Esay. 38." (Isa. 38).

16. Steward.

17. Later, this emphasis on remembering all of one's sins lessens, and some ecclesiastics even begin to regard it as unnecessary. See Bautista, *Advertencias*, fols. 1:2v–5v.

In beginning your life you need to start from your childhood, to remember what you did when you were still a little child, when you began to understand things a bit, when you were able to reason, and then when you were a young man, and then a mature man, and an old man in what ways you offended our lord. Also remember when you married and when you were given some duty—whether rulership, governorship, judgeship, or something else that became your honored duty—whether in it you offended our lord! And also you are to remember what you did wrong when you became a widower or widow, or when you were prosperous or poor, or when you were sick. Also, when you had confrontations among yourselves and you were hating one another, or you were becoming friends with someone.

And remember if you were doing something in artisanry, or you were a trader so that you will remember well each time that in that way you took advantage of someone so that you mistreated someone. And remember each sin you committed on Sunday and on days to be observed or on major church holidays. Perhaps you did not keep well each of the days that was your obligation, and perhaps you did not hear mass, and perhaps during vigils or Lent you did not fast or you ate meat? In the same way remember all the places you lived and those you lived next to and how many you became friends with and how many you lived next to, who helped you in your making a living, whom perhaps you helped and knew, whether they provoked you or you provoked them concerning sin!

Also remember all your bad thoughts, bad intentions, bad desires with which you viewed someone with disgust, anger, you hated someone, you coveted someone, you wanted someone to die; with which you wanted to avenge yourself on someone so that you really wanted revenge on your tormenter, and each time that you envied someone! And it is necessary that you remember all that you did wrong with your mouth and tongue. Perhaps you said something bad about God and his saints, or you mentioned the name of our lord in vain. Perhaps you made up something about someone, gave false testimony about someone, you fooled someone. Perhaps you dishonored someone, or you murmured against someone behind his back, or perhaps you caused trouble and spread dissension amid those with whom you lived. Perhaps dirty, bad, and vain words came from your mouth.

Also remember each sin that you committed, that you fully completed and carried out, so that you stole something, you took something from someone, you snatched something from someone, carried it off, or you have invested someone else's property for interest, taking a field or house, etc. And remember each time you have been in concubinage or committed adultery! Or you committed some other unmentionable sin with which you dirtied yourself. It is necessary for you to examine yourself closely so that you will confess all your blackness and filthiness and all your disgusting pleasures. However, it is necessary for you to be very careful with the memory of disgusting pleasure so that you do not dwell on it for a long time, so that you will never dirty yourself with it again. Just recount it quickly, go right past it, but remember it well so that you can present it to a priest.

And you are to remember and examine yourself on each commandment of our lord God and the commandments of our mother, the Holy Church. And you will remember if you made light of one of the Holy Church's sacraments she holds, and it is your obligation to receive it so that you will be saved. Perhaps you fell into a deadly sin, and perhaps you did not firmly believe all of the Articles of Faith that our mother, the Holy Church, commands you with all rigor to believe. Perhaps you sometimes doubted one and perhaps you undervalued it many times and many times did not receive the Holy Spirit's gift gladly, and you did not do all the good things he was inspiring in you and reminding you of. Perhaps you did not do the fourteen mercies that belong to the soul and the flesh. Perhaps you did not take care of your five perceptions (senses) relating to your flesh. And perhaps you did not live each of the purifying virtues called theological and cardinal; three are called theological: faith, hope, and divine charity. And four cardinal: fortitude, temperance, rectitude, and prudence. This, then, is what is very necessary for you to remember calmly before you confess. And also remember well how each time you committed a deadly sin, and how much time you were committing it, or you desired to sin and really would do it if it were feasible, if you could, if something did not prevent you.

Second, so that your confession will be perfect, it is necessary for you to remember and do some other things when you are about to confess. First, it is necessary for you to confess and acknowledge well your sins and not just cover up something. If you hid something from the confessor, when you confessed once, it is counted as nothing because you only spoiled your confession. Therefore, it is necessary for you to now tell your sins you hid and the rest that you said to the confessor when you confessed before him. And if you confessed two or three times and if likewise the same number of times you hid one or two of your sins, you need to tell again all the rest of your sins before those two or three priests; again you will take it and start from the beginning when you hid one or two of your sins.

Nor can you blame your sins on something so that you will not be shamed, but you are to face it head on and really shame yourself over it. You will not say, "The devil forced me to sin." Nor are you to say, "It is my friend or my relative that made me sin and provoked me so that I sinned." Nor are you to say, "I did it contrary to my will but my flesh forced me, or my spouse, or my relative." You will not say, "But they gave me pulque[18] so that I became drunk; I did not buy it for myself, nor request it. As for the meat I ate Friday, Sunday, and during Lent or the four liturgical seasons or vigils I did not cook it nor eat it in my home." Never talk that way, but you are to say, "Voluntarily, I ate or drank that what I should not eat or drink, because I accepted it when it was given to me, and it was my own fault because I should not obey the person who persuaded me to sin and provoked me to go against our lord's commandments. Although I should have died at the hands of the person tempting me, I should not have approved what he said and obeyed him. That is the way it was, because I was responsible for what I did and committed and my foolish action."

Also you are not to say, "Nor am I in the slightest able to restrain myself concerning my concubinage, my drinking, or my robbing because I am not strong enough in order to restrain myself." But you are to say, "It is very true that I wanted to sin; if I had not wanted to, I would not have sinned, and our lord God would have helped me by his grace so that I would not fall into deadly sin, into which I fell voluntarily, and by my will I desired it. And because I desired it, right away I did it."

In addition, it is necessary for you to confess with very great humility. There, you will show no arrogance, boasting, or self-praise, and never ever is a lie to emerge from your mouth before a priest.

18. Pulque is a fermented alcoholic beverage made from the maguey plant.

Nor are you to make up stories about yourself or others, but you are to confess very truthfully and humbly. And it is necessary for you that you confess for the sake of our lord God so that really only voluntarily will you obey him and please him and so that with purity you will serve him when all your sins have disappeared through confession.

You will not confess principally in order to free yourself from hell, or so that your soul and body will obtain help, or so that you will go to have great rejoicing in heaven. But you are to confess principally so that you please, obey, and honor the one deity God who surpasses all in deserving to be pleased, obeyed, and entirely loved. And you are to have great confidence in him; you are to say, "Truly he will help me, he will pardon me of all my sins so that I will forever belong to him and be close to him and so that I will praise him forever among all the angels and saints. And because of this, may I cast down all my sins before a priest. As if I were sick, let me reveal to the physician all my sicknesses. And as if I were poor, let me tell of all my poverty to my ruler and to him who enriches me so that he will take pity on me and cure me and give me wealth and abundance."

In addition, it is necessary for you to tell only sins that you committed yourself, or how you caused another person to sin. You are not to tell someone else's sins as it is not necessary for you to speak ill of someone in the confessional, or name whom you sinned together with, although it is very much your obligation to name the person with whom you sinned, or the person who sinned with you, if the person is your relative or kin, etc. And it is necessary for you to confess voluntarily, not by force or intimidation. Because nothing you do merely because of force and not performed voluntarily will please our lord God.

Also, it is very necessary for your confession to be complete. You are to say absolutely everything you did wrong in your mind and in your words, and what you did in actions, or what you did wrong in your mind and in action. You are to leave out nothing at all. And you are not to divide up your confession, but you will tell every one of your sins to a single priest, one who understands your language well and who is especially prudent and fears our lord God and who likewise has the authority to absolve you of all your sins. And although our lord God knows all your sins, it is very necessary for you yourself to declare it truly and say it now before a priest, because our lord God wants you yourself to say it all and to humble yourself and shame yourself so that through your humility you will obtain pardon for your sins.

And it is necessary for you to confess secretly before only one priest. You are to inform only one priest of your sins, not many at once. Nor are neighbors or associates to be listening, either male or female. In addition, it is necessary for you to tell your sins with weeping and tears; you are to mention them with sighs. With great sorrow and repentance you will recount your wickedness so that the Lord of the Near and Close and the Giver of Life will pardon you, as in the scriptures you have heard many times of how God forgave very great sinners because of their weeping and their tears with which before him they wept and grieved.

And it is necessary for you not to delay your confession, nor are you to go along putting it off so that you do not put your soul in danger. Because if you confess after a long time, you will forget very many of your sins; no longer will you be able to remember it all when you want to confess, for which reason if you are able to do it, do not confess only during Lent but confess many times throughout the year.

In addition, it is necessary for you that your confession be very strong so that you hide absolutely none of your sins or keep your silence out of embarrassment or fear; for no reason whatever are you to slight your confession, although you consider it very difficult how to make restitution and how to return someone's honor to them or the penance that the priest will give to you or how you are to reject completely the bad life you were comfortable with and how you will begin anew and devote yourself fully to a good life. But especially now you should make every effort in order to obey your deity and ruler, God, and your mother, the Holy Church, and so that you will have great pity on and help your soul. You are to fully affirm and carry out entire obedience to our lord Jesus Christ's representative, the priest, in whatever he should order you. And if he should assign you something very difficult to do, plead with him to give you another penance that you feel you can do. And declare the reason for which it is not possible for you to do the difficult thing that he had ordered you. Say, "O my Father! Because of my illness, or a great task that I am working at, it is not possible for me to do what you want of me. Have pity on me by your life so that I can merely favor the sick and the blind, give them a little something, or I will serve for a few days in the hospital, etc."

Third, in order that our lord God can be merciful to you, it is very necessary for you to change your life and set forth decidedly to no longer commit sins and offend your deity and ruler, God. And it is necessary that you restore and return to others their honor if you should have disgraced someone. And you should appease others and appease yourself concerning the sorrow you received from one another. In addition, it is necessary for you to perform and carry out what I now order you, the penance.

And if you will do all three things I have mentioned, our lord God will truly be merciful on you, and he will pardon you of all your sins, and your soul will greatly rejoice and be consoled. And you will live peacefully in the world of our lord God, and in many things you will be enriched and you will enjoy because of your soul's purity obtained through its confession, as the great learned man Saint Augustine declares to you when he speaks about confession's glory and honor. He says, "Through spiritual confession—called sacramental confession—all the bad in someone's life is destroyed and he/she attains full strength and all goodness and kindness, the virtues, and becomes wholly deserving and good, and with it (the confession) all the demons are defeated, fooled, and scorned, and it is great comfort and medicine for sinners. And I say that confession really closes the mouth of hell, and really opens all the doors of heaven." These are exactly the words of Saint Augustine.[19]

And Saint Gregory also marvels at how confession is good, admirable, and marvelous. He says, "May everyone admire and greatly esteem those who go about guarding themselves, who live chastely, and who wholly scorn disgusting pleasures and those who cultivate a peaceful life. And also, may those servants of our lord God be admired who live justly so that their justice, mercy, and compassion are perfect. As for me, however, I am astounded beyond measure by those who humbly confess, who acknowledge their sins."[20] For these

19. In the column is "August de vera & falsa poenitentia." (Augustine, *De vera et falsa poenitentia*). This work was popular reading throughout the Middle Ages, and although it was often erroneously ascribed to Saint Augustine, as it is here, the author is in fact unknown. Le Goff, *Birth of Purgatory*, 364–65.

20. In the column is "Gregorus ad regem Vngarie." (Gregory to the king of Hungary).

reasons Saint Augustine says, "O my precious younger siblings![21] Confess and acknowledge your sins. Do not delay your confession for anything so that you will be able to completely satisfy your souls and give them substance here on the earth through our lord's grace, and afterward for that very reason you will be able to attain glory, eternal rejoicing in heaven. Amen."[22]

Here are given the questions that will be asked of people before the confession begins.

O my precious child, tell me! Were you able to remember and find all your sins? Did your blackness, your filthiness, and all your wickedness with which you offended your deity and ruler cause you to weep and grieve? Are you strongly determined to sin no more? Do you really want to change your life so that no more will you offend the Giver of Life? Were you baptized? Did you voluntarily receive God's holy water called baptism? Perhaps you merely thought of it as a joke, or they dragged you along to be baptized?

Have you married, or are you still single? In what way do you earn your living? What is your work? In what way do you obtain what you need? Have you confessed another time, or is now the first time that you are confessing? When, how long ago, did you confess? How many times have you confessed? Have you been excommunicated for something? How did you fall on (incur) it? For what reason was it decreed upon you? When you confessed, were you embarrassed or frightened? Did you conceal some of your sins? Did you do the penance which the father ordered for you because of your sins? Were you going to restore someone's property and did not? Or you were to flagellate yourself, or fast, or count your beads, or show favor to the poor and did not do it? Did you forget it, or voluntarily because of laziness omit it and neglect it, or go along putting it off and delaying it?

If the person confessing says he already did his penance, then let the priest say to him, "Say the *Persignum crucis* and the confession (General Confession)."[23]

---

21. A metaphor referencing the audience.

22. In the column is "August ad fratr. in hęre serm. 20" (Augustine to the Brothers, sermon 20).

23. The General Confession, or the Confiteor, was a prayer that established the general formula of the confession itself. Penitents were to recite the General Confession prior to their confession.

General Confession

Unworthy I, a sinner, I, a great sinner, confess before God and also holy Mary, forever truly virgin, and Saint Peter; Saint Paul; Saint Michael, the archangel; Saint Francis; and all the saints that live in heaven, and also before you, father, for I sinned through eating, drinking, with laughter, frivolities, taking pleasure in others' misfortunes, wrong words, and carnal living; I cannot change my life. Finally, I was going to do good things, but I did not; I was going to abandon all that is not good, but I did not. Because of that my heart weeps before God. I say, "I sinned, I sinned, I sinned greatly," yet now I entirely reject the devil, and I give myself entirely to our lord God. I also implore holy Mary, forever truly virgin, great implorer for people, to pray to her precious child, Jesus Christ, on my behalf to forgive me all my sins and be merciful to me. And I implore you, father, at the order of our lord God, absolve me!

Excerpt from *Breve práctica* (1761), Copied by Manuel Joseph de Reyna (1770)

Brief and abridged banishment of the most commonly known misunderstandings of the Indians, that inasmuch as experience teaches, that from continual conversation with them, many sins that they commit by mistaken awareness are avoided; I supplicate the learned ministers of the holy sacraments, and the most exact and vigilant parish priests of the Mexican Indians, that, excusing my own, before the high mass in their respective churches of the parishes they govern, that they order to have read to the Indians this very short treatise.

O my children! Understand that it is necessary that we bow low only before our God, only before him will we bend our knees, and we will serve only him, and there is nothing else with which we can worship, because a person cannot worship [him] with residents of hell, with mud-children,[24] with snakes, metates, or with other things

---

24. From *zoquicoconeme*, likely in reference to or the equivalent of the Tlaloque—the attendants of the rain god, Tlaloc—who lived in the mountains, among other places. These prominent deities were the source of many headaches among ecclesiastics, as they were the deities many natives continued to invoke—even today!—to ensure rain for their harvest. An example is provided in the text, where Velázquez informs natives that they commit a mortal sin when they believe in a *quieuhtlazqui*, "a conjuror of rain," or a *teziuhtlazqui*, "a conjuror of hail."

to confuse people with which the hell-demon, the devil, tempts and confuses indigenous people, by which he makes them fall into mortal sin through serving him. If some Christian is confused, it is necessary that he immediately change his mind and confess about it; if not, he cannot be saved and our deity cannot pardon him.

Likewise, indigenous people will confess at that time if they incite their friends with some confusion and teach them bad things, whether with wrong beliefs or with carnal living or with thievery, whether they are adults or children, and they commit as many sins as the people they incite; because, if you incite four people, you commit four deadly sins. And although you do not incite them, if you commit mortal sin in front of them so that in front of someone you did it, you will confess and you will say how many people [you did it] in front of.

Also, understand that there are many things in which you burden yourselves with mortal sin unthinkingly, and this is my duty to which our deity appointed me; I desire and look into the salvation of your souls. Wherefore, I am speaking to and advising you that on Ash Wednesday those who are authentically indigenous people are not to fast because there is no command for indigenous people to fast on that day; the only obligation for indigenous people is to fast nine days in an entire year: one on the vigil of the birth of our lord Jesus Christ called Noche Buena (Christmas Eve), seven fasts on the seven Fridays of Lent, and another on the Sábado de Gloria (the Saturday before Easter). Thus, it is not necessary for an indigenous person to say in confession that he did not fast on Ash Wednesday, because he is to know that fast is not his obligation.

Likewise, it is announced that old men and old women, those who are already sixty years old no longer are obliged to fast. Likewise, sick people, those who have an abdominal illness, and those who have stomach pains or some other head ailment, even though they go about the altepetl (i.e., are ambulatory), are not obliged to fast. Thus, if they omit them (the fasts), it is not necessary for them to confess about it. Likewise, birthing women and those who are nursing and raising children, because that is hard work, are not obligated to fast. Likewise, those men who work all day or suffer from traveling on the road, and those who hunt all day or all night, are not obliged to fast; nor youth and maidens not yet twenty-one are not yet obliged to fast. Likewise, indigenous people are not obliged to attend mass on Ash Wednesday because it is not their obligation; likewise on a

Novena mass indigenous people do not sin if they miss the Novena masses; wherefore it is not necessary for them to confess.

Indigenous people cannot eat meat during Lent or Ash Wednesday or on Sunday, because during all of Lent they are to observe vigils and cannot eat meat, even on Sábado de Gloria, but yes, sick people can eat meat, those who are lying sick on mats, whether it be women, men, or maidens or youths, and if they are sick with an abdominal, stomach, or head illness it is not a sin if they eat meat, although they go about the altepetl as was already said about fasting, and even on Good Friday they can eat meat. Likewise, those who are healthy cannot eat meat on all vigils for the whole year. On Friday, on Saturday, yes they can eat meat if it does not fall on a vigil; and birthing women and those who are nursing and raising children and those who are pregnant and the old men and old women already sixty years old and children, whether young male or female, not yet seven years old can eat meat.

Healthy Christians cannot eat duck on vigils, during Lent, on Friday, but yes, they are able to eat it on Saturday, and likewise small children who count as seven years old cannot eat meat if they are healthy, on Lent, Fridays, or vigil, and they are already obliged to see Sunday mass on that day. Likewise, those who are sick, lying sick on mats, and those who cannot go about are not obliged or required [to see] mass whether on Sunday or on the feast days that are observed; concerning birthing women they do not commit sin when they skip mass during the one month they are caring for themselves and recovering. Thus, it is not necessary for them to confess regarding the missed mass when they were birthing women.

An indigenous person commits mortal sin if he believes what a deceiver, a conjurer of rain and conjurer of hail tells him; likewise a conjurer of rain performs a mortal sin when he undertakes that task and deceives indigenous people, because he cannot conjure rain, he does not have the power of our deity; only priests alone have the power through their priesthood our deity gave to them so that they can destroy and defeat the rainstorm and hail, and those living things that damage fields called locusts.[25]

---

25. On occasion, ecclesiastics would attempt to use their authority to rebuke the winds and banish storms, primarily through the use of a saint. In 1737 the archbishop of Mexico invoked the Virgin of Guadalupe to end the current epidemic—

When a indigenous person confesses, after he has knelt down, right then he is to cross himself and declare with all his heart the Act of Contrition, oh my deity, and he is to relate, to present that which is true; he cannot hide the sin he keeps inside his heart, and he cannot claim what is not his sin. Likewise, he cannot lie when he begins his confession, he cannot say that he has no sin, for the distracter, the devil, he likewise confuses when he begins to confess; he commits a sin by lying. Thus, he should not say that he has no sin.

The confession should first begin with the sins of the penitent and let him be afraid of lying, let him get his memory straight and with truthfulness separately tell and declare all his sins, because he commits a terrible mortal sin if he does not first search his mind for all his sins so that he remembers everything he sinned in and, thus, with truthfulness declares them all.

Likewise, if he knows some enchantment or has used one, he is to confess it; even though someone, no matter who, tells him to hide it, because if he hides it or omits it from shame, even with his fear he commits a terrible mortal sin and the confession is spoiled, and our deity will give him a great punishment. If the indigenous person believes a dream right at the time when he is sleeping, he does not sin; if he believes a dream when he is awake, when he is already alert, at that time, yes, he commits a terrible mortal sin.

And understand that when you confess, it is not necessary for you to say the names of your sins, it is not necessary for their names to be made known. Likewise, it is not necessary, and there is not a requirement, for you to fast on the day you confess; concerning this, understand that you did not fast when you confessed.

Understand also that compadres through baptism and likewise through confirmation cannot get married (to each other). Compadres through blessings, saint blessings, can get married because they are not true compadres, they do not become relatives. However, understand that when a youth is seeking a wife he cannot go to work in the home of that woman; likewise, a woman cannot go to work in the house of the man; let each one be inside his/her own home so that they will not encounter the deception of the demon of hell, the devil, mortal sin. When they have married then they will become companions, they will be together inside their house so that they will not encounter that which is bad.

And likewise it is necessary that the indigenous person understand that he does not commit mortal sin when he drinks although he enjoys half a real's worth of white pulque, because he cannot lose his judgment by enjoying half a real's worth of white pulque. This includes any person on earth, and because there are official orders that only half a real's worth of white pulque a day can be sold each day to an indigenous person from inside the hut from which it is sold, called the place of selling pulque, *pulquería*.

Furthermore, it is also not necessary for you to confess that you drank half a real's worth (of white pulque) in one day; or when you drink a bit of it, although you drink it every day, it is not a great sin if with it you do not hurt your earthly body. Wherefore hear it well so that every year you do not become confused, or at the moment you confess, that you only commit mortal sin when you drink too much and because of it you lose your judgment, fall on the earth, lose control of your body, and when you do not remember what you do.

When you do not drink too much, you do not commit mortal sin, although you vomit on yourself, although you drink every day;[26] and when you drink too much you commit only one mortal sin from drunkenness, when you vomit on yourself, and it is necessary that you fear the terrible mortal sin that you incur when you are drunk before many people, because you commit as many sins as there are people before whom you sin, whether your wife, your children, or other relatives of yours and when you are drunk remember and know that you declare frivolous words and insults, perhaps you kill someone. Understand that you assume all these sins when you begin to drink!

Also, it is necessary that you understand that when you commit small thefts, like tortillas, maize dough, wheat bread, an egg, a bit of salt, a bit of meat, or a bit of nixtamal (maize soaked in lime water), even if it should be worth half a real, it is not a mortal sin. It is only a mortal sin, and you will assume it, when you steal one real from your fellow indigenous person because there at the Tolucan plains he works all day in order to earn one real. And if an indigenous person

---

26. That Velázquez spends time to excuse the drinking (albeit tempered) of the natives is extraordinary, as native drunkenness was one of the more common complaints among ecclesiastics.

earns two reales in one day, then you commit mortal sin if you take or steal from him two reales; one real or one and a half real, you commit a small sin. But if that person is very poor, although you take merely half a real, you commit a terrible mortal sin because with that half a real he was going to be able to eat that day. And if that person is a Spaniard or an indigenous person with great belongings who has much property, if you take or steal from him one peso you will commit a terrible mortal sin in this kingdom. But if you seize or take from this one two reales, four, six, or seven and a half reales, you commit only a small sin.[27]

Understand well what I say to you, that way you will always fully understand what is required of you. Likewise, understand that you commit as many sins as there are people present when you steal. Wherefore, through this my admonition all you indigenous people can avoid many sins, because you will know and understand well what deeds are not sins, and you will set your own lives in order. May our deity wish it to be so.

Excerpt from Juan Coronel, *Confessionario breve*, in *Discursos predicables* (1620), fols. 232v–236r

Small confessional manual for confessing the Indians

Put the ordinary questions in the language (Maya) and Spanish according to the sins they usually commit, and in which they ordinarily sin and is asked of them.

The following is that which is to be asked of the penitent before he relates his sins, after crossing himself and saying the Confession (Confiteor).
When did you (last) confess your sins, declare your sins?
Did you tell all your sins to the priest?
Perhaps there are sins you hid from the priest when you confessed?
Perhaps there are sins you forgot when you confessed?

27. As previously stated, eight reales equaled one peso. Here, the gravity of the sin is not based so much on what is stolen, but its value in comparison to the financial situation of the owner.

Did you complete what the priest told you?

Does it pain you, your sin against God, the Ruler?

Do you give your spirit (dedicate yourself) to never sin against God again?

Tell all your sins without hiding one.

Allow him to say his sins, and according to what he might say, he is asked the circumstances of them, and if he does not say them, the following is asked of him.

Concerning the commandments of the law of God

1. *Love God.*

Do you love God above all things?

Perhaps you have believed your dreams, or the cries of birds?

2. *You will not swear.*

Perhaps you swore in the name of God, like "Deity[28] knows," while lying?

You knew you were lying?

What lie did you say?

3. *Honor the feast days.*

Perhaps you have worked on Sundays, or on feast days assigned to you all to observe?

What was the work you did?

Did you work the entire day?

And have you permitted your children and your family to work?

4. *Honor* [your] *father and mother.*

Perhaps you have despised your father and your mother?

Perhaps you have nicknamed them "devils" or something similar?

5. *You will not kill.*

Perhaps you have desired the death of someone, or misfortune to come upon your neighbor?

---

28. Although the text typically employs the Spanish "Dios" for "God," here the Maya *ku* is used. The Mayas employed *ku* as a standard term for "deity," and although it occasionally appears in the context of the Christian god, it also frequently appears in reference to Maya deities. Thus, I translate it as "deity" to distinguish it from the Catholic Dios.

6. *You will not fornicate.*
Perhaps you have sinned with some woman (*if it is a man; and if it is a woman*), with some man?
How many people?
How many times with one, and what of the other one?
Did he have a woman/man?[29] (Were the partners single or married?)
They were your relatives, perhaps?
How are they related to you?
They are relatives, perhaps, of your husband/your wife?
How are they related to him/her?
Perhaps you have desired some woman/man?
How many people?
How many times did you desire them?
They were your relatives, perhaps?
Did you have the inclination to sin with them?
Perhaps you have pleasured yourself/touched yourself immodestly?

7. *You will not steal.*
Perhaps you have stolen?
What did you steal?
How many things did you steal?
How much was it worth?
Did you know the owner?
Was it returned to the owner?

8. *You will not give* [false] *testimony.*
Perhaps you have given a false accusation or you defamed the reputation of your neighbor?
What accusation did you speak about him?

The Commandments of the Holy Mother Church
To hear mass.
Perhaps you have neglected mass on Sunday or on the feast days, the guarded days assigned to you all?
How many times did you neglect mass?

---

29. Occasionally, as in this instance, the manual inserts components that refer directly to a male or female penitent. I place both components together, divided here and throughout with a slash.

What is the reason you neglected it?
Where were you when you neglected it?
Perhaps you were healthy?
What did you do?
Perhaps you have ceased to send your children to see mass on
Sundays?

To eat meat.
Perhaps you have eaten meat on Friday or on Saturday or during
Lent or on the other days of fasting?
How many times did you eat it?
Perhaps you were healthy?
Where were you?
Perhaps you had food?
Perhaps you had companions?
You, perhaps, were the reason they ate?

To get drunk.
Perhaps you have been drunk?
How many times?
You lost, perhaps, your will when you were drunk?
You fell, perhaps, on the ground?
Perhaps you have drunk balche?[30]
Perhaps you have incited someone to sin?
Perhaps you have summoned some mistress?

---

30.   Balche is a fermented drink made from honey and the bark of the balche tree.
The drink was commonly used in Maya rituals and continued in use throughout the
colonial period.

Acuña, René. "Escritos mayas inéditos y publicados hasta 1578: Testimonio del obispo Diego de Landa." *Estudios de Cultura Maya* 21 (2001): 165–71.

Alighieri, Dante. *Dante's Inferno: The Indiana Critical Edition*. Edited and translated by Mark Musa. Bloomington: Indiana University Press, 1995.

Alva, Don Bartolomé de. *A Guide to Confession Large and Small in the Mexican Language, 1634*. Edited by Barry D. Sell and John Frederick Schwaller with Lu Ann Homza. Norman: University of Oklahoma Press, 1999.

Andrien, Kenneth, ed. *The Human Tradition in Colonial Latin America*. Wilmington, Del.: Scholarly Resources, 2002.

Austern, Linda Phyllis, Kari Boyd McBride, and David L. Orvis, eds. *Psalms in the Early Modern World*. Surrey: Ashgate, 2011.

Baldwin, Deborah J. *Protestants and the Mexican Revolution: Missionaries, Ministers, and Social Change*. Urbana: University of Illinois Press, 1990.

Barnes, Monica. "Catechisms and Confessionarios: Distorting Mirrors of Andean Societies." In *Andean Cosmologies Through Time: Persistence and Emergence*, ed. Robert V. H. Dover, Katharine E. Seibold, and John H. McDowell, 67–94. Bloomington: Indiana University Press, 1992.

Baudot, Georges. *Utopia and History in Mexico: The First Chroniclers of Mexican Civilization, 1520–1569*. Translated by Bernard R. Ortiz de Montellano and Thelma Ortiz de Montellano. Niwot: University Press of Colorado, 1995.

Bautista, fray Juan. *Advertencias para los confesores de los naturales*. 2 vols. Mexico City: Melchor Ocharte, 1600. Reproduced in Hernández de León-Portilla, *Obras clásicas*.

———. *A Iesu Christo S. N. ofrece este sermonario en lengua mexicana*. Mexico City: Diego Lopez Daualos, 1606. Reproduced in Hernández de León-Portilla, *Obras clásicas*.

———. *Huehuetlahtolli*. Mexico City: Convento de Santiago Tlatilulco, Ocharte, 1600.

Beristáin de Souza, José Mariano. *Biblioteca hispanoamericana septentrional (1816)*. Vol. 3. Mexico City: Universidad Nacional Autónoma de México, 1980.

Bolles, David. Transcription of *Discursos predicables*. Foundation for the Advancement of Mesoamerican Studies. http://www.famsi.org/reports/96072/corodoctorg.pdf.

Bricker, Victoria R., and Helga-María Miram, eds. and trans. *An Encounter of Two Worlds: The Book of Chilam Balam of Kaua.* New Orleans: Tulane University Middle American Research Institute, 2002.

Bristowe, Lindsay W., and Philip B. Wright. *The Handbook of British Honduras for 1888–1889.* London: Blackwood and Sons, 1888.

Burkhart, Louise M. *Before Guadalupe: The Virgin Mary in Early Colonial Nahuatl Literature.* Austin: University of Texas Press, 2001.

———. "Death and the Colonial Nahua." In Sell and Burkhart, *Death and Life,* 29–54.

———. "'Here Is Another Marvel': Marian Miracle Narratives in a Nahuatl Manuscript." In *Spiritual Encounters: Interactions Between Christianity and Native Religions in Colonial America,* ed. Nicholas Griffiths and Fernando Cervantes, 91–115. Lincoln: University of Nebraska Press, 1999.

———. *Holy Wednesday: A Nahua Drama from Early Colonial Mexico.* Philadelphia: University of Pennsylvania Press, 1996.

———. "The 'Little Doctrine' and Indigenous Catechesis in New Spain." *Hispanic American Historical Review* 94, no. 2 (forthcoming).

———. *The Slippery Earth: Nahua-Christian Moral Dialogue in Sixteenth-Century Mexico.* Tucson: University of Arizona Press, 1989.

———. "The Voyage of Saint Amaro: A Spanish Legend in Nahuatl Literature." *Colonial Latin American Review* 4, no. 1 (1995): 29–57.

Canadé Sautman, Francesca, Diana Conchado, and Giuseppe Carlo Di Scipio, eds. *Telling Tales: Medieval Narratives and the Folk Tradition.* New York: St. Martin's Press, 1998.

Caso Barrera, Laura. *Chilam Balam de Ixil: Facsmiliar y estudio de un libro maya inédito.* Mexico City: Artes de México y del Mundo, 2011.

Christensen, Mark Z. *Nahua and Maya Catholicisms: Texts and Religion in Colonial Central Mexico and Yucatan.* Stanford: Stanford University Press; Berkeley: Academy of American Franciscan History Press, 2013.

———. "The Tales of Two Cultures: Ecclesiastical Texts and Nahua and Maya Catholicisms." *The Americas* 66, no. 3 (2010): 353–77.

———. "The Teabo Manuscript." *Ethnohistory* 60, no. 4 (2013): 788–89.

———. "The Use of Nahuatl in Evangelization and the Ministry of Sebastian." *Ethnohistory* 59, no. 4 (2012): 691–711.

Christian, William A. *Local Religion in Sixteenth-Century Spain.* Princeton: Princeton University Press, 1981.

Chuchiak, John Franklin, IV. "Pre-conquest *Ah Kinob* in a Colonial World: The Extirpation of Idolatry and the Survival of the Maya Priesthood in Colonial Yucatán, 1563–1697." In Hostettler and Restall, *Maya Survivalism,* 135–60.

———. "Secrets Behind the Screens: Solicitantes in the Colonial Diocese of Yucatan and the Yucatec Maya, 1570–1785." In *Religion in New*

Spain, ed. Susan Schroeder and Stafford Poole, 83–109. Albuquerque: University of New Mexico Press, 2007.

Cline, S. L., and Miguel León-Portilla, eds. *The Testaments of Culhuacan*. Nahuatl Studies 1. Los Angeles: UCLA Latin American Center, 1984.

Códice franciscano, siglo XVI: Nueva colección de documentos para la historia de México. Mexico City: Editorial Salvador Chávez Hayho, 1941.

Cogolludo, Diego López de. *Historia de Yucatán*. Madrid: García Infanzón, 1688.

Corcuera de Mancera, Sonia. *El fraile, el indio, y el pulque: Evangelización y embriaguez en la Nueva España (1523–1548)*. Mexico City: Fondo de Cultura Económica, 1991.

Coronel, fray Juan. *Arte en lengua de maya: Y otros escritos*. 1620. Edited by René Acuña with appendixes by David Bolles. Mexico City: Universidad Nacional Autonóma de México, 1998.

———. *Discursos predicables, con otras diuersas materias espirituales, con la doctrina xpna, y los articulos de la fé*. Mexico City: Pedro Gutiérrez en la Emprenta de Diego Garrido, 1620.

Domínguez y Argáiz, Francisco Eugenio. *Pláticas de los principales mysterios de nvestra Sta fee con una breve exortación al fin del modo con que deben excitarse al dolor de las culpas*. Mexico City: Colegio de Ildefonso, 1758.

Don, Patricia Lopes. *Bonfires of Culture: Franciscans, Indigenous Leaders, and Inquisition in Early Mexico, 1524–1540*. Norman: University of Oklahoma Press, 2010.

Dover, Robert V. H., Katharine E. Seibold, and John H. McDowell, eds. *Andean Cosmologies Through Time: Persistence and Emergence*. Bloomington: Indiana University Press, 1992.

Early, John D. *Maya and Catholic Cultures in Crisis*. Gainesville: University Press of Florida, 2012.

———. *The Maya and Catholicism: An Encounter of Worldviews*. Gainesville: University Press of Florida, 2006.

Étienne de Besançon. *An Alphabet of Tales: An English Fifteenth-Century Translation of the Alphabetum narrationum of Etienne de Besançon*. Vol. 2. Edited by Mary Macleod Banks. London: Paul, Trench, Trübner, 1904–5.

Farriss, Nancy M. *Maya Society Under Colonial Rule: The Collective Enterprise of Survival*. Princeton: Princeton University Press, 1984.

Fernández del Castillo, Francisco. *Libros y libreros en el siglo XVI*. Mexico City: Archivo General de la Nación, Fondo de Cultura Económica, 1982.

Findlay, George Gillanders, and William West Holdsworth. *The History of the Wesleyan Methodist Missionary Society*. Vol. 2. London: Epworth Press, 1921.

[Fletcher, Richard]. *Catecismo de los metodistas. No. 1, para los niños de tierna edad. Catecismo ti le metodistaoob. No. 1, utial mehen palaloob*. London, 1865.

Flos sanctorum. Castile, ca. 1472–75.

Gayangos, Pascual de. *Escritores en prosa anteriores al siglo XV*. Vol. 51 of *Biblioteca de autores españoles*. Madrid: Rivadeneyra, 1860.

George-Hirons, Amy. "Tell Me, Maiden: The Maya Adaptation of a European Riddle Sequence." *Journal of Latin American Lore* 22, no. 2 (2005): 125–42.

Gibson, Charles. *The Aztecs Under Spanish Rule: A History of the Indians of the Valley of Mexico, 1519–1810*. Stanford: Stanford University Press, 1964.

Glass, John. "A Census of Native Middle American Pictorial Manuscripts." In *Guide to Ethnohistorical Sources*. Vol. 14 of *Handbook of Middle American Indians*, ed. Robert Wauchope, 81–252. Austin: University of Texas Press, 1975.

Gómez de Orozco, Federico. *Catálogo de la colección de manuscritos relativos a la historia de América*. Mexico City: Secretaria de Relaciones Exteriores, 1927.

Gómez de Parada, Juan. *Constituciones sinodales del obispado de Yucatán*. Edited by Gabriela Solís Robleda. Mérida: Universidad Nacional Autónoma de México, 2008.

Gregory, Saint. *Dialogues*. Translated by Odo John Zimmerman, OSB. New York: Fathers of the Church, 1959.

Griffiths, Nicholas, and Fernando Cervantes, eds. *Spiritual Encounters: Interactions Between Christianity and Native Religions in Colonial America*. Lincoln: University of Nebraska Press, 1999.

Gruzinski, Serge. *Man-Gods in the Mexican Highlands: Indian Power and Colonial Society, 1520–1800*. Translated by Eileen Corrigan. Stanford: Stanford University Press, 1989.

Hanks, William F. *Converting Words: Maya in the Age of the Cross*. Berkeley: University of California Press, 2010.

Hernández de León-Portilla, Ascensión, comp. *Obras clásicas sobre la lengua náhuatl*. Fuentes lingüísticas indígenas 8. Madrid: Fundación Histórica Tavera, 1999. CD-ROM.

Homza, Lu Ann. "The European Link to Mexican Penance: The Literary Antecedents to Alva's *Confessionario*." In Alva, *Guide to Confession*, 33–48.

Horcasitas, Fernando. *El teatro náhuatl: Épocas novohispana y moderna*. Mexico City: Universidad Nacional Autónoma de México, 1974.

Hostettler, Ueli, and Matthew Restall, eds. *Maya Survivalism*. Markt Schwaben, Germany: Verlag Anton Saurwein, 2001.

Hull, Kerry M., and Michael D. Carrasco, eds. *Parallel Worlds: Genre, Discourse, and Poetics in Contemporary, Colonial, and Classic Maya Literature*. Boulder: University Press of Colorado, 2012.

Jacobus de Voragine. *The Golden Legend*. Ca. 1260. Translated by Christopher Stace. New York: Penguin, 1998.

Jacques de Vitry. *The Exempla, or Illustrative Stories from the Sermones Vulgares*. Edited by Thomas Frederick Crane. London: Nutt, 1890.

Johnson, Wallace R. *A History of Christianity in Belize, 1776–1838*. Lanham: University Press of America, 1985.

Karttunen, Frances. *Between Worlds: Interpreters, Guides, and Survivors*. New Brunswick, N.J.: Rutgers University Press, 1994.

Knowlton, Timothy. "Dynamics of Indigenous Language Ideologies in the Colonial Redaction of a Yucatec Maya Cosmological Text." *Anthropological Linguistics* 50, no. 1 (2008): 90–112.

———. *Maya Creation Myths: Words and Worlds of the Chilam Balam*. Boulder: University Press of Colorado, 2010.

Kutscher, Gerdt, Gordon Brotherston, and Günter Vollmer, eds. *Aesop in Mexico: Die Fabeln des Aesop in aztekischer Sprache*. Berlin: Gebrüder Mann Verlag, 1987.

Landa, fray Diego de. *Landa's relación de las cosas de Yucatan: A Translation*. Translated by Alfred M. Tozzer. Papers of the Peabody Museum 18. Cambridge: Peabody Museum of American Archaeology and Ethnology, Harvard University, 1941. Reprint, Millword, N.Y.: Kraus, 1975.

Le Goff, Jacques. *The Birth of Purgatory*. Chicago: University of Chicago Press, 1984.

León-Portilla, Miguel. *Aztec Thought and Culture: A Study of the Ancient Nahuatl Mind*. Translated by Jack Emory Davis. Norman: University of Oklahoma Press, 1978.

———. *Bernardino de Sahagún, First Anthropologist*. Norman: University of Oklahoma Press, 2002.

———. *Huehuetlahtolli: Testimonios de la antigua palabra*. Mexico City: Secretaría de Educación Pública/Fondo de Cultura Económica, 1991.

Lockhart, James. *The Nahuas After the Conquest: A Social and Cultural History of the Indians of Central Mexico, Sixteenth Through Eighteenth Centuries*. Stanford: Stanford University Press, 1992.

Lorenzana, Francisco Antonio. *Concilios provinciales primero, y segundo, celebrados en la muy noble y muy leal ciudad de México, presidiendo el Illmo. Y Rmo. Señor D. Fr. Alonso de Muntúfar, en los años de 1555, y 1565*. Mexico City: Imprenta del Superior Gobierno, Hogal, 1769.

Maire Bobes, Jesús, ed. *Cuentos de la edad media y del siglo de oro*. Madrid: Ediciones Akal, 2002.

Mathes, W. Michael. *The America's First Academic Library: Santa Cruz de Tlatelolco*. Sacramento: California State Library Foundation, 1985.

Mendieta, fray Jeronimo de. *Historia eclesiástica indiana*. 2 vols. Madrid: Atlas, 1973.

Molina, fray Alonso de. *Confessionario breue, en lengua mexicana y castellana*. Mexico City: Espinosa, 1565.

————. *Confesionario mayor en la lengua mexicana y castellana (1569)*. Mexico City: Instituto de Investigaciones Filológicas, Instituto de Investigaciones Históricas, Universidad Nacional Autónoma de México, 1984.

Molina Solís, Juan Francisco. *Historia de Yucatán durante la dominación española*. 3 vols. Mérida: Imprenta de la Lotería del Estado, 1904–13.

Morgan, Ronald J. *Spanish American Saints and the Rhetoric of Identity, 1600–1810*. Tucson: University of Arizona Press, 2002.

Mosquera, Daniel. "Nahuatl Catechistic Drama: New Translations, Old Preoccupations." In Sell and Burkhart, *Death and Life*, 55–84.

Motolinia (Benavente), fray Toribio de. *Memoriales o libro de las cosas de la Nueva España y de los naturales de ella*. Edited by Edmundo O'Gorman. Mexico City: Instituto de Investigaciones Históricas, Universidad Nacional Autónoma de México, 1971.

Nesvig, Martin Austin. *Forgotten Franciscans: Writings from an Inquisitional Theorist, a Heretic, and an Inquisitional Deputy*. University Park: Pennsylvania University Press, 2011.

————. *Ideology and Inquisition: The World of the Censors in Early Mexico*. New Haven: Yale University Press, 2009.

Pardo, Osvaldo F. *The Origins of Mexican Catholicism: Nahua Rituals and Christian Sacraments in Sixteenth-Century Mexico*. Ann Arbor: University of Michigan Press, 2004.

Paredes, Ignacio de. *Promptuario manual mexicano*. Mexico City: Bibliotheca Mexicana, 1759. Reproduced in Hernández de León-Portilla, *Obras clásicas*.

Parker, Margaret. *The Story of a Story Across Cultures: The Case of the Doncella Teodor*. London: Tamesis, 1996.

Pérez de Ribas, Andrés. *History of the Triumphs of Our Holy Faith Amongst the Most Barbarous and Fierce Peoples of the New World*. Translated by Daniel T. Reff, Maureen Ahern, and Richard K. Danford. Tucson: University of Arizona Press, 1999.

Pettas, William. *A Sixteenth-Century Spanish Bookstore: The Inventory of Juan de Junta*. Philadelphia: American Philosophical Society, 1995.

Phelan, John L. *The Millennial Kingdom of the Franciscans in the New World*. 2nd ed. Berkeley: University of California Press, 1970.

Pizzigoni, Caterina. *Testaments of Toluca*. Nahuatl Studies 8. Stanford: Stanford University Press, 2006.

Poole, Stafford, CM. *Our Lady of Guadalupe: The Origins and Sources of a Mexican National Symbol, 1531–1797*. Tucson: University of Arizona Press, 1995.

Ramos, Gabriela. *Death and Conversion in the Andes: Lima and Cuzco, 1532–1670*. Notre Dame: University of Notre Dame Press, 2010.

Restall, Matthew. *The Black Middle: Africans, Mayas, and Spaniards in Colonial Yucatan*. Stanford: Stanford University Press, 2009.

————. "Gaspar Antonio Chi: Bridging the Conquest of Yucatán." In *The Human Tradition in Colonial Latin America*, ed. Kenneth Andrien, 6–21. Wilmington, Del.: Scholarly Resources, 2002.

————. *Life and Death in a Maya Community: The Ixil Testaments of the 1760s*. Lancaster: Labyrinthos Press, 1995.

————. *The Maya World: Yucatec Culture and Society, 1550–1850*. Stanford: Stanford University Press, 1997.

Ricard, M. L'Abbé Antoine. *The Twelve Months Sanctified by Prayer: November, Month of the Souls in Purgatory*. London: Washbourne, 1877.

Ricard, Robert. *The Spiritual Conquest of Mexico: An Essay on the Apostolate and the Evangelizing Methods of the Mendicant Orders in New Spain, 1523–72*. Translated by Lesley Byrd Simpson. Berkeley: University of California Press, 1966.

Ripalda, Gerónimo de. *Catecismo mexicano*. Translated and edited by Ignacio de Paredes. Mexico City: Bibliotheca Mexicana, 1758.

Roeber, A. G. "The Waters of Rebirth: The Eighteenth Century and Transoceanic Protestant Christianity." *Church History* 79, no. 1 (2010): 40–76.

Roys, Ralph L. *The Titles of Ebtun*. Washington, D.C.: Carnegie Institution of Washington, 1939.

Rugeley, Terry. *Maya Wars: Ethnographic Accounts from Nineteenth-Century Yucatán*. Norman: University of Oklahoma Press, 2001.

————. *Of Wonders and Wise Men: Religion and Popular Cultures in Southeast Mexico, 1800–1876*. Austin: University of Texas Press, 2001.

————. *Yucatán's Maya Peasantry and the Origins of the Caste War*. Austin: University of Texas Press, 1996.

Ruiz de Alarcón, Hernando. *Treatise on the Heathen Superstitions That Today Live Among the Indians Native to This New Spain, 1629*. Translated and edited by J. Richard Andrews and Ross Hassig. Norman: University of Oklahoma Press, 1984.

Ruz, fray Joaquin, trans. *Colección de sermones para los domingos de todo el año, y cuaresma*. Mérida: Espinosa, 1846.

Sáenz de la Peña, Andrés. *Manual de los santos sacramentos*. Mexico City: Robledo, 1642. Reproduced in Hernández de León-Portilla, *Obras clásicas*.

Sahagún, fray Bernardino de. *Coloquios y doctrina cristiana*. Translated and edited by Miguel León-Portilla. Mexico City: Universidad Nacional Autónoma de México/Fundación de Investigaciones Sociales, 1986.

————. *Introductions and Indices*. Part 1 of *Florentine Codex: General History of the Things of New Spain*. Translated and edited by Arthur J. O. Anderson and Charles E. Dibble. Santa Fe, N.M.: School of American Research; Salt Lake City: University of Utah Press, 1982.

————. *Psalmodia christiana*. 1583. Translated and edited by Arthur
J. O. Anderson. Salt Lake City: University of Utah Press, 1993.

Sam Colop, Luis Enrique. "Poetics in the *Popol Wuj*." In *Parallel Worlds:
Genre, Discourse, and Poetics in Contemporary, Colonial, and Classic Maya Literature*, ed. Kerry M. Hull and Michael D. Carrasco,
283–309. Boulder: University Press of Colorado, 2012.

Sánchez de Aguilar, Pedro. *Informe contra idolorum cultores de obispado de
Yucatán*. 1636. 3rd ed. Mérida: Triay e Hijos, 1937.

Sánchez de Vercial, Clemente. *The Book of Tales by A. B. C.* Translated
and edited by John E. Keller, L. Clark Keating, and Eric M. Furr.
New York: Lang, 1992.

Sautman, Francesca Canadé, Diana Conchado, and Giuseppe Carlo Di Scipio.
Telling Tales: Medieval Narratives and the Folk Tradition. New York:
St. Martin's Press, 1998.

Scanlon, Larry. *Narrative, Authority, and Power: The Medieval Exemplum
and the Chaucerian Tradition*. Cambridge: Cambridge University
Press, 1994.

Schroeder, H. J. *The Canons and Decrees of the Council of Trent*. Saint
Louis: Herder, 1941.

Schwaller, John F. "The Pre-Hispanic Poetics of Sahagún's *Psalmodia
christiana*." In *Psalms in the Early Modern World*, ed. Linda Phyllis Auster, Kari Boyd McBride, and David L. Orvis, 315–32. Surrey:
Ashgate, 2011.

Sell, Barry D. "The Classical Age of Nahuatl Publications and Don Bartolomé de Alva's *Confessionario* of 1634." In Alva, *Guide to Confession*,
17–32.

————. "Friars, Nahuas, and Books: Language and Expression in Colonial
Nahuatl Publications." PhD diss., University of California, Los Angeles, 1993.

————. "Nahuatl Plays in Context." In Sell and Burkhart, *Death and Life*,
3–28.

Sell, Barry D., and Louise M. Burkhart, eds. *Death and Life in Colonial
Nahua Mexico*. Vol. 1 of *Nahuatl Theater*. Norman: University of
Oklahoma Press, 2004.

————. *Nahuatl Theater*. 4 vols. Norman: University of Oklahoma Press,
2004–9.

Silverstein, Theodore. *Visio Sancti Pauli: The History of the Apocalypse in
Latin, Together with Nine Texts*. London: Christophers, 1955.

Sousa, Lisa, Stafford Poole, CM, and James Lockhart, trans and eds.
The Story of Guadalupe: Luis Laso de la Vega's "Huei tlamahuiçoltica" of 1649. Stanford: Stanford University Press/UCLA Latin
American Center, 1998.

Tavárez, David. *The Invisible War: Indigenous Devotions, Discipline, and
Dissent in Colonial Mexico*. Stanford: Stanford University Press,
2011.

———. "Naming the Trinity: From Ideologies of Translation to Dialectics of Reception in Colonial Nahua Texts, 1547–1771." *Colonial Latin American Review* 9, no. 1 (2000): 21–47.

Taylor, William. *Magistrates of the Sacred: Priests and Parishioners in Eighteenth-Century Mexico*. Stanford: Stanford University Press, 1996.

Thompson, Philip C. *Tekanto, a Maya Town in Colonial Yucatan*. New Orleans: Tulane University Middle American Research Institute, 1999.

Tozzer, Alfred M. *A Maya Grammar*. Cambridge: Peabody Museum of American Archaeology and Ethnology, Harvard University, 1921. Reprint, New York: Dover, 1977.

Tubach, Frederic C. *Index Exemplorum: A Handbook of Medieval Religious Tales*. Helsinki: Suomalainen Tiedeakatemia, 1969.

Vázquez Gastelu, Antonio. *Arte de lengua mexicana*. Mexico City: Imprenta de Fernandez de León, 1689. Reproduced in Hernández de León-Portilla, *Obras clásicas*.

Velázquez de Cárdenas y León, Carlos Celedonio. *Breve práctica y régimen del confessonario* [sic] *de indios en mexicano y castellano*. Mexico City: Imprenta de la Bibliotheca Mexicana, 1761.

Wesleyan Methodist Church in Canada. *The Catechisms of the Wesleyan Methodists . . . No. 1, for Children of Tender Years*. Toronto: Rose, 1866.

Wesleyan Methodist Connection of America. *Doctrines and Disciplines of the Wesleyan Methodist Church*. Ann Arbor: Sullivan, 1842.

The Wesleyan Missionary Notices, Relating Principally to the Foreign Missions. Methodist Conference, vol. 10, no. 3. London: Nichols, 1863.

Whalen, Gretchen. "An Annotated Translation of a Colonial Yucatec Manuscript: On Religious and Cosmological Topics by a Native Author." Foundation for the Advancement of Mesoamerican Studies, 2002. http://www.famsi.org/reports/01017.

Wright, Elizabeth R. "A Dramatic Diaspora: Spanish Theater and Its Mexican Interpretation." In *Spanish Golden Age Drama in Mexican Translation*. Vol. 3 of *Nahuatl Theater*, ed. Barry D. Sell, Louise M. Burkhart, and Elizabeth R. Wright, 3–25. Norman: University of Oklahoma Press, 2008.

latin american originals

Series Editor | Matthew Restall

This series features primary source texts on colonial and nineteenth-century Latin America, translated into English, in slim, accessible, affordable editions that also make scholarly contributions. Most of these sources are being published in English for the first time and represent an alternative to the traditional texts on early Latin America. The initial focus is on the conquest period in sixteenth-century Spanish America, but subsequent volumes include Brazil and examine later centuries. The series features archival documents and printed sources originally in Spanish, Portuguese, Latin, and various Native American languages. The contributing authors are historians, anthropologists, art historians, and scholars of literature.

Matthew Restall is Edwin Erle Sparks Professor of Colonial Latin American History, Anthropology, and Women's Studies, and Co-Director of Latina/o, Latin American, and Caribbean Studies, at the Pennsylvania State University. He is an editor of *Ethnohistory*.

Board of Editorial Consultants
J. Michael Francis (chair)
Jane G. Landers | Kris Lane
Laura E. Matthew | Martin Austin Nesvig

Titles in print

*Invading Colombia: Spanish Accounts of the
Gonzalo Jiménez de Quesada Expedition of Conquest* (LAO 1)
J. Michael Francis

Invading Guatemala: Spanish, Nahua, and Maya Accounts of the Conquest Wars (LAO 2)
Matthew Restall and Florine G. L. Asselbergs

*The Conquest on Trial: Carvajal's "Complaint of the Indians
in the Court of Death"* (LAO 3)
Carlos A. Jáuregui

*Defending the Conquest: Bernardo de Vargas Machuca's
"Defense and Discourse of the Western Conquests"* (LAO 4)
Edited by Kris Lane and Translated by Timothy F. Johnson

*Forgotten Franciscans: Works from an Inquisitional Theorist, a Heretic,
and an Inquisitional Deputy* (LAO 5)
Martin Austin Nesvig

*Gods of the Andes: An Early Jesuit Account of Inca Religion
and Andean Christianity* (LAO 6)
Sabine Hyland

Of Cannibals and Kings: Primal Anthropology in the Americas (LAO 7)
Neil L. Whitehead